The FBI Files
on
ELVIS PRESLEY

Volumes in the TOP SECRET
series by
New Century Books:

World War Two:
U.S. Military Plans for the Invasion of Japan

The FBI Files on Elvis Presley

TOP SECRET

The FBI Files
on
ELVIS PRESLEY

Thomas Fensch, Editor

New Century Books

New Century Books
P.O. Box 7113
The Woodlands, Tx., 77387-7113

Library of Congress Number: 20011117308
ISBN #:   Hardcover   0-930751-03-5
               Softcover   0-930751-04-3

Contents

Introduction

Elvis Presley never committed a crime.

Elvis Presley was never accused of any crime.

But for decades the FBI kept a file on Presley, not for anything he did, but for threats made against him; complaints about his public performances; an extortion attempt; mention of a paternity suit; the theft by larceny of an executive jet he owned and the alleged fraud (subsequently proven untrue) involving the sale of a 1955 Corvette he had bought new.

These behind-the-scenes files show dramatically how the FBI had to react to others involved in Presley's world; how J. Edgar Hoover replied to citizen complaints; and how the Washington, D.C. headquarters of the FBI and field offices throughout the United States worked — often with other government law enforcement agencies — to prosecute individuals involved with crimes surrounding Presley.

In some cases, the work of the FBI and other agencies was fruitless — when death threats were received on handwritten postal cards, the FBI was unable (in the cases cited in this file) to find the writer of such threats. In other cases, such as the theft by larceny of Presley's executive jet, individuals were accused of, and prosecuted for that crime.

In the case of the extortion threat by Laurens Johannes Griessel-Landau, material in the FBI files came from U.S. Military officials in Europe, alerted to the case by Presley himself.

These documents represent over 650 pages of

FBI files in Washington DC. Other government law enforcement agencies may well have their own files about crimes against Presley; in his home town of Memphis, in Las Vegas and Los Angeles, perhaps (and even elsewhere). The extent of files about crimes against Presley, located outside the files of the FBI may never be known.

The files in these pages represent, in microcosm, the behind-the-scenes life of any major national or international rock star, and other national or international entertainers. These files could well be duplicated time after time, under the name of other stars, national politicians, government leaders and, certainly in the case of death threats, against each modern President of the United States.

As a *caveat* to the reader: these files were originally photocopied from FBI records, then stored on a CD-Rom. The files were then reprinted from the CD-Rom; commentary and analysis by the editor was added, then the manuscript was retyped and electronically coded for publication by "print-on-demand" technology.

Every effort has been made to retain the accuracy of these files; no changes have been made by the editor, save to clarify, whenever possible, material that appeared garbled.

Neither the editor nor New Century Books is responsible for any errors due to this chain of photocopying, CD-Rom storage, reprinting and eventual publication in book form.

These files show the thrust of activity against Elvis Presley throughout the years and the efforts of the FBI to react to these threats, complaints and crimes.

These files represent the raw history of our times.

The files reflect one individual, who became internationally known, and who changed not only our culture, but affected the entire western world. The files, however, represent the dark side of international fame; a side little-known to fans of Presley and his music, yet perfectly understandable to those in law enforcement and those behind the scenes in the entertainment world and in other facets of public life.

Incidents and cases in these FBI files act as a sober *caveat* for us all, entertainers as well as those who love them.

As an added advisory to the reader: before declassifying these formerly secret documents, the FBI has chosen to delete certain words, phrases, names, addresses, paragraphs and even whole pages of documents. Samples of the deletions (*redactions*, in legalese, meaning *getting ready for publication*) appear in the Appendix. Reasons for omitting material are not given, except for codings related to certain types of secrecy classifications.

Additional names, addresses, paragraphs, and pages related to Elvis Presley may still remain secret. The extent of any such continued secret documents is also unknown.

— *Thomas Fensch*

The FBI Files on Elvis Presley

The earliest set of documents in the Presley file is correspondence dated March and April, 1959 regarding a death threat made when Presley was serving in the U.S. Army in Germany. "SAC" is "Special Agent in Charge" of an FBI Bureau. (Copies of the letter about the threat, which is almost illegible, are in the Appendix):

TO: DIRECTOR, FBI
ATT: FBI LABORATORY

FROM: SAC, NEW YORK (62-12152)

SUBJECT: ELVIS-PRESLEY
           INFORMATION CONCERNING

Enclosed herewith are the original and a Photostate of a letter dated 3/11/59, and the envelope postmarked 3/12/59, addressed to RCA VICTOR RECORDS, 155 East 24th Street, NY 10, NY, which contains information from an anonymous writer that plans had been made for a Red Army soldier to kill ELVIS PRESLEY, well-known entertainer, who is presently stationed in US Army in Germany.

Legal Department, RCA, who made letter available on 3/19/59, advised that it had been received 3/16/59, and was handled by numerous people on the staff. Stated that PRESLEY'S manager, Col. THOMAS PARKER, Box 417, Madison, Tenn., phone # Nashville 8-2858, was informed of contents of letter and he advised that letter appeared identical to letters received in past from a woman in Ohio and that FBI had already looked into matter. PARKER stated woman was "nuts." Letter contained no personal threats from writer.

Two Photostats are being forwarded for assistance of Memphis Office and it is requested that Memphis instruct Laboratory as to what action desired.

Date: April 22, 1959
To: Assistant Chief of Staff for Intelligence
Department of the Army
The Pentagon
Washington 25, D. C.

From: John Edgar Hoover, Director
Federal Bureau of Investigation

Subject: ELVIS PRESLEY
INFORMATION CONCERNING

Attached is a Photostat of an anonymous letter dated March 11, 1959; postmarked Canton, Ohio, and addressed to RCA Victor Records, 155 East 24th Street, New York 10, New York, which contains information to the effect that a Red Army soldier in East Germany is planning to kill Elvis Presley, a well-known entertainer, presently attached to the U. S. Army in Germany.

Legal Dept., RCA, has advised that the contents of this letter have been made available to Presley's manager, Colonel Thomas Parker, Madison, Tennessee. For your information, during 1957 and 1958, one wrote several threatening letter to Presley. Voluntarily entered the ??, an institution for mental patients, at . The Assistant U. S. Attorney at Cleveland, Ohio, declined prosecution of for violation of the Extortion Statute in view of her mental condition.

The handwriting on the enclosed letter was examined by the FBI Laboratory and it was concluded that the handwriting was not identical with that of known specimens by

6

The above is being forwarded you for your information and so further investigation will be conducted by this Bureau.

REPORT
Of the
FBI
LABORATORY
WASHINGTON, D. C.

To: FBI, New York

Re: ELVIS PRESLEY
       INFORMATION CONCERNING

Date: April 14, 1959
FBI File No. 3-3064
Lab No.   303175 DG

Specimens received 3/25/59

Envelope postmarked "CANTON OHIO MAR 12, 1959 2:30 PM," addressed to "R. C. A. Victor Records 155 E. 24th St New York 10 New York," and accompanying four-page letter dated 3/11/59, beginning "Dear Sir" I have just . . . ." and ending " . . . . Thank You."

Result of examination:

Specimen Q1 was searched through the appropriate sections of the Anonymous Letter File without effecting an identification. Copies of this material are not being added to this file unless future developments warrant such action.

It was concluded that specimen Q1 was not prepared by whose known handwriting has been designated as specimen K3 in the case entitled ELVIS PRESLEY, VICTIM, EXTORTION.

Specimen Q1 is being retained in the files of

the Bureau.

Also one of the very earliest documents in the FBI files about Elvis Presley is a letter dated April 11, 1956 from Memphis, Tennessee, protesting Presley's immoral behavior:

Mr. J. Edgar Hoover, Director
Federal Bureau of Investigation
Washington, D. C.

Dear Mr. Hoover:

By way of introduction to you, will say that I knew (x) when he was in Memphis, and thought a great deal of him. Believe he will remember me, in our association together on occasions.

Am attaching a few clippings for your perusal. They are sent to indicate a trend with which you may already be familiar.

It is essential that some agency with sufficient organization and influence do something toward better censorship in our country. There are minds who will scarcely stop short of complete indecency to explicit their wares upon the public, and youth is not able to discriminate between the right and wrong of it.

We have had a struggle here on the local front in Memphis, a city of 455,000 people, in retaining a censorship, when a committee appointed had suggested that it was not necessary.

Have personally talked with members on the local censorship board, and have their testimony of the terrible pictures that would be released for showing here, had it not been for censorship.

Most of this entertainment becomes interstate, and hence should become a Federal Government problem. The fine work that our Churches and some of our schools are attempting to do is offset by the freedom exercised in this country of licentiousness. The Apostle Peter warned in his 1st letter about our not using the new liberty for a cloke of maliciousness, but as the servants of God.

If there is something that your excellent and very fine organization is able to do concerning these problems facing us today, you will find that many citizens will deeply appreciate your effort.

May I take this occasion to thank you most sincerely for your own exemplary record and for preserving a great America for us at the risk of your life and that of your agents.

Cordially yours,

A letter in reply from J. Edgar Hoover's desk had to remind that citizen that the F.B.I. was not a moral watchdog for the country, an image that Hoover himself had generated and nurtured for decades.

April 17, 1956

Mr.
Memphis, Tennessee

Dear Mr.

Your letter of April 11, 1956, and its enclosures have been received, and I can appreciate the concern which prompted your writing. I would like to advise you, however, that the FBI is strictly a fact-gathering agency, and it is not within the scope of our authority to make suggestions as to legislative matters.

I am most grateful for your generous remarks concerning the FBI and assure you of our desire always to merit your confidence.

Sincerely yours,

John Edgar Hoover
Director

A letter on the letterhead of the newspaper published by the Catholic diocese of La Crosse, Wisconsin, dated May 16, 1956, complained about Presley's immoral behavior in a local appearance. The writer claimed "There is also gossip of the Presley Fan Clubs that degenerate into sex orgies" and "I would judge that he may possibly be both a drug addict and a sexual pervert." The writer also claimed that Presley's performances were "serious to U.S. security." The writer remained convinced that "juvenile crimes of lust and perversion will follow his show here in La Crosse."

Mr. J. Edgar Hoover
Director
Federal Bureau of Investigation
Washington 25, D. C.

Dear Mr. Hoover,

Elvis Presley, press-agented as a singer and entertainer, played to two groups of teenagers numbering several thousand at the city auditorium here, Monday, May 14.

As newspaper man, parent, and former member of Army Intelligence Service, I feel an obligation to pass on to you my conviction that Presley is a definite danger to the security of the United States.

Although I could not attend myself, I sent two reporters to cover his second show at 9;30 p.m. besides, I secured the opinions of others of good judgment, who had seen the show or had heard direct reports of it. Among them are a radio station manager, a former motion picture exhibitor, an orchestra player, and a young woman employee of a radio station who witnessed the show to determine its value. All agree that it was the filthiest and most harmful production that ever came to La Crosse for exhibition to teenagers.

When Presley came on the stage, the youngsters almost mobbed him, as you can judge from the article and pictures enclosed from May 15 edition of the La Crosse TRIBUNE. The audience could not hear his "singing" for the screaming and carrying on of the teenagers.

But eye-witnesses have told me that Presley's

actions and motions were such as to rouse the sexual passions of teenaged youth. One eye-witness described his actions as "sexual self-gratification on the stage," — another as "a strip-tease with clothes on." Although police and auxiliaries were there, the show went on. Perhaps the hardened police did not get the import of his motions and gestures, like those of masturbation or riding a microphone. (The assistant district attorney and Captain William Boma also stopped in for a few minutes in response to complaints about the first show, but they found no reason to halt the show.)

After the show, more than 1,000 teenagers tried to gang into Presley's room at the auditorium, then at the Stoddard Hotel. All possible police on duty were necessary at the Hotel to keep watch on the teenagers milling about the hotel till after 3 a.m., the hotel manager informed me. Some kept milling about the city till about 5 a.m.

Indications of the harm Presley did just in La Crosse were the two high school girls (of whom I have direct personal knowledge) whose abdomen and thigh had Presley's autograph. They admitted that they went to his room where this happened. It is known by psychologists, psychiatrists and priests that teenaged girls from the age of eleven, and boys in their adolescence are easily aroused to sexual indulgence and perversion by certain types of motions and hysteria, — the type that was exhibited at the Presley show.

There is also gossip of the Presley Fan Clubs that degenerate into sex orgies. The local radio station WKBH sponsors a club on the "Lindy

Shannon Show."

From eye-witness reports about Presley, I would judge that he may possibly be both a drug addict and a sexual pervert. In any case I am sure he bears close watch, — especially in the face of growing juvenile crime nearly everywhere in the United States. He is surrounded by a group of high-pressure agents who seem to control him, the hotel manager reported.

I do not report idly to the FBI. My last official report to an FBI agent in New York before I entered the U.S. Army resulted in arrest of a saboteur (who committed suicide before his trial). I believe the Presley matter is as serious to U.S. security. I am convinced that juvenile crimes of lust and perversion will follow his show here in La Crosse.

I enclose article and pictures from May 15 edition of the La Crosse TRIBUNE. The article is an excellent example of the type of reporting that describes a burlesque show by writing about the drapes on the stage. But the pictures, to say the least are revealing. Note, too, that under the Presley article, the editor sanctimoniously published a very brief "filler" on the FBI's concern for teenage crime. Only a moron could not see the connection between the Presley exhibit and the incidence of teenage disorders in La Crosse.

With many thanks, and with a prayer for God's special blessing on your excellent and difficult work for justice and decency,

Sincerely yours,

J. Edgar Hoover's office had to explain that the F.B.I. did not have jurisdiction in the matter raised by the La Crosse writer:

La Crosse Register
Post Office Box 822
La Crosse, Wisconsin

Dear Mr.

Your letter dated Apr. 10, 1956, with enclosures, has been received.

While I appreciate the interest prompting you to write, the matter to which you refer is not within the investigative jurisdiction of the FBI.
I want to thank you, however, for your most generous remarks relative to the work of this Bureau.

Sincerely yours,

John Edgar Hoover
Director

In early November, 1956, the Louisville Bureau filed a report via radio that local police officials were afraid that riots might break out at the Kentucky State Fair, as both Presley and Bill Haley and His Comets were both booked and were "RIVALS FOR THE ATTENTION OF QUOTE ROCK AND ROLL UNQUOTE FANS":

DECODED COPY

Radio Teletype

FROM LOUISVILLE   11-7-56   MR 071428

TO DIRECTOR   URGENT

Elvis Presley; Bill Haley and His Comets, information concerning, police cooperation matter. Colonel Carl E. Heustis, Chief of Police, Louisville, Kentucky, this day advised that Elvis Presley and Bill Haley and His Comets, rivals for the attention of quote rock and roll unquote fans, are simultaneously booked for appearances at the Jefferson County Armory and the Kentucky State Fairground Exposition Center November 25 Next. Colonel Heustis advised he has received information that there have been riots at Jersey City, New Jersey, Asbury Park, New Jersey, Santa Cruz, Santa Jose, California, Hartford, Connecticut, and Jacksonville, Florida as result of such simultaneous appearances. Riots reportedly resulted in many thousands of dollars property damage. Colonel Heustis requested information from this bureau regarding any such riots in an effort to prevent such recurrences here. In view of the excellent cooperation between Louisville PD and this office it is requested that the bureau furnish an airtel summary of any information appearing in files suitable for dissemination to Colonel Heustis.

Received: 11:05 AM Radio

          11:22 AM CODING UNIT

TOP SECRET

The following top paragraph is Hoover's reply to Louisville. The "NOTE" material at the bottom of the file is apparently a briefing for Hoover, to aid him in forming a reply.

11-7-50

AIRTEL

SAC, Louisville

ELVIS PRESLEY;
BILL HALEY AND HIS COMETS;
INFORMATION CONCERNING
POLICE COOPERATION MATTER

Your radiogram 11-7-56, in which you request information in Bureau files concerning disturbances which occurred following appearances of above subjects. While the Bureau is aware that newspaper articles reported riots and disturbances following appearances of the above individuals no inquires have been made and the Bureau has no specific information regarding these disturbances. Since Colonel Heustis is aware of the places where riots allegedly occurred you may desire to tactfully suggest that he consult with the chiefs of police in those localities for any information in this regard.

Hoover

RFS:jdn
(4)

NOTE: Louisville was contacted by Colonel Heustis, Chief of Police, Louisville, Kentucky, who advised of the coming appearances of above subjects and his fear of the riots as occurred in sev-

eral other cities. As a matter of cooperation
Colonel Heustis requested information from this
Bureau regarding these riots. Louisville is being
advise that while the Bureau is aware that such
riots have occurred no inquiries were made and
we have no specific information concerning these
riots. It is being suggested to the SAC, Louisville,
that he may desire to suggest to Colonel Heustis
that he consult with chiefs of police in the cities
where the riots occurred.

In September, 1956, a postal card was sent to Presley in Memphis, stating only:

IF YOU DON'T STOP THIS SHIT, I'M GOING TO KILL YOU

The SAC in Buffalo, New York was alerted as the postal card was mailed from the Buffalo area. Identification of the writer could not be made and federal officials in Buffalo decided that the card was sent from a "crank." The following is part of the SAC's report from Buffalo dated September 17, 1956:

NO 9-531

The above measure on the postal card was written in pencil and is printed.

By letter dated September 20, 1956, the FBI Laboratory advised that the hand-printing on the postal card in question was reached through the anonymous letter file without identifying it with a prior submission.

On September 17, 1956, the facts of this case were discussed with Assistant United States Attorney RICHARD E. MOOT at Buffalo, New York, who advised that in the event the identity of the unsub was obtained, he should decline prosecution inasmuch as the card appears to be from a "crank." Mr. MOOT further advised, however, that in the event additional threatening cards or letters are received by the victim, he should be advised and additional consideration would be given him to the prosecution of the person involved.

It is being pointed out that the complete text of the message on the postal card, including the obscene word, was furnished to Mr. MOOT.

A monthly intelligence report about politics in Mexico, sent to the FBI from an FBI LEGAT (Legal Attache), Mexico, March 11, 1957, observes how Presley's supposedly racial comments had been received in Mexico. (These comments appears to be so contrived as to be propaganda for the Mexican film in question.)

ROCK AND ROLL

Mexican magazines and newspapers have for months pointed out that the vogue for rock and roll dancing among the youth in the United States was a sign of moral degeneration perfectly explainable in the United States, but not present in Mexico. It was said that the new dance rhythm would find no popular reception among the Mexican youth due to their strict upbringing and serious views toward life. Then rock and roll began to catch on. Considerable money was even invested in a locally made movie in which certain prominent Mexican entertainers danced and otherwise approved of the craze. At that time a news report reached Mexico City that during a radio interview in Los Angles ELVIS PRESLEY had made a statement that he would rather kiss three Negresses rather than one Mexican girl. This reported statement has received tremendous publicity, so much so that it would almost appear contrived. A campaign has been successfully initiated to prevent the playing of any ELVIS PRESLEY recording over any Mexican City radio station, and on March 14 next university students are planning a protest celebration in a downtown Mexico City park where ELVIS PRESLEY music, magazines, and recordings will be publicly burned. The Communists, quick to ban rock and roll dancing from Mexican Communist youth social functions, may try to spark the bonfire meeting in the plaza, but even the Communists may not stop rock and roll in Mexico. The new ads for the aforementioned movie point out that

Mexican rock and roll is an independent dance of local origin. The ad reads: "Death to ELVIS PRESLEY! Burn his records, his pompadour, his photographs, his guitar, burn anything you want, but give yourself a treat with the true kings of happiness and of rock and roll!" At last reports the movie was receiving extremely good attendance.

One of the saddest episodes on file with the FBI is a short-two page report by a Provost Marshall Major Warren H. Metzner. Apparently when Presley was in the military service in Germany, he hired a man proported to be a medical doctor and a skin specialist.

Laurens Johannes Griessel-Landau extorted sums of money from Presley; Presley apparently reported the extortion to military authorities. Presley was cleared of any wrong-doing and Griessel-Landau apparently left Germany.

Approximately 18 pages of Griessel-Landau's handwritten letters appear in the FBI files.

Two reports on the incident follow:

Office Memorandum • UNITED STAGES GOVERN-
MENT

TO: DIRECTOR, FBI

FROM: LEGAT, BONN (64-859)

SUBJECT: Changed:
 LAURENZ JOHANNES IN GRIESSEL-LAN-
DAU
 POLICE COOPERATION
 FOREIGN MISCELLANEOUS

The title in this case has been changed to
reflect the correct name of the subject as reported by the Provost Marshal Division.

Rebucable to Bonn 12/30/59, entitled "LAU-
RENCY LANDAU, PCFM."

Information concerning the subject was furnished to this office by the Provost Marshal
Division, Hqs., U.S. Army, Europe, with the indication that they wished to avoid any publicity in
this matter since they did not want to involve
ELVIS PRESLEY nor put him in an unfavorable
light since PRESLEY had been a first-rate soldier
and had caused the Army no trouble during his
term of service. The information furnished by the
Provost Marshal Division in a self-explanatory
memorandum classified For Official Use Only is
enclosed. Seven Photostats of letters from GRIES-
SEL-LANDAU to PRESLEY or to one of PRESLEY'S
secretaries are also enclosed.

Foregoing is provided for information purposes.

MEMORANDUM   5 February 1960

Elvis Presley was interviewed on 28 December 1959 concerning his complaint that he was the victim of blackmail by a Mr. Laurens Johannes GRIESSEL-LANDAU, of Johannesburg, South Africa. GRIESSEL-LANDAU represents himself to be a doctor specialist in the field of dermatology. GRIESSEL-LANDAU is not a medical doctor.

Copies of letters from GRIESSEL-LANDAU to Presley and Presley's private secretary were obtained on loan basis so that they could be photographed.

On or about 27 November 1959, GRIESSEL-LANDAU appeared at the residence of Elvis Presley in Bad Nauheim, Germany and began his treatments. These treatments took place in Presley's quarters in the presence of two female secretaries (both U. S.). The treatment involved Presley's shoulders and face.

Presley reports that GRIESSEL-LANDAU made several homosexual advances to some of his enlisted friends. GRIESSEL-LANDAU also is alleged to have admitted to Presley that he is bisexual. His first homosexual experiences took place early in his life in the orphanage in which he was brought up.

On 24 December 1959 Presley decided to discontinue the skin treatments. At the time that he told GRIESSEL-LANDAU of this decision he also thoroughly censured GRIESSEL-LANDAU for embarrassing him as a result of the improper advances that he (GRIESSEL-LANDAU) made to his (Presley's) enlisted friends. GRIESSEL-LAN-

DAU immediately went into a fit of rage, tore up a photo album of Presley's, and threatened to ruin his singing career and to involve Presley's American girl friend (a 16 year old daughter of an Air Force captain). GRIESSEL-LANDAU further threatened to expose Presley by photographs and tape recordings which are alleged to present Presley in compromising situations. Presley assures me that this is impossible since he never was in any compromising situations. Presley contends that GRIESSEL-LANDAU is mentally disturbed. This is based upon the fits GRIESSEL-LANDAU has had and on his statements concerning the shock treatments he has been taking . .

By negotiation, Presley agreed to pay GRIESSEL-LANDAU $200.00 for treatments received and also to furnish him with a $315.00 plane fare to London, England. GRIESSEL-LANDAU agreed to depart to England on 25 December 1959 at 1930 hours from Frankfurt, Germany. GRIESSEL-LANDAU did not leave as agreed, rather returned and demanded an additional $250.00, which Presley paid. A day later GRIESSEL-LANDAU made a telephonic demand for 2,000 ß for the loss of his practice which he closed in Johannesburg, South Africa prior to his departure for Bad Nauheim to treat Presley.

GRIESSEL-LANDAU finally departed Rhein-Main Air Field, Frankfurt, Germany at 1600 hours, 6 January 1960 on Flight 491, British European Airway for London, England under the name of GRIESSEL. He is alleged to be seeking entry into the United States. No contact between Presley and GRIESSEL-LANDAU has been reported since 5 January.

WARREN E. METZNER
Major, MPC
Chief, Investigations Branch

FOR OFFICIAL USE ONLY

In early 1964, Presley was again the focus of a death threat. A postal card was mailed from Huntsville, Alabama, Jan. 10, 1964 to:

Presdient Elvis Presly
Memphis S, Tennessee

And stated:

You Will Be
Next On My
List

The postal card also mentioned country singer Johnny Cash, a "Tommy" (unclear), President "JBJ" (presumably Lyndon Baines Johnson), and George C. Wallace. Since the "JBJ" was close to L.B.J., the post card was assumed to also be a threat to the president and treated as such. (A copy of the postal card appears in the Appendix.) The writer of the postal card could not be identified by the FBI Laboratory in Washington, but the possible threat to Lyndon Baines Johnson was passed along to the Secret Service.

REPORT
of the
FBI
LABORATORY

FEDERAL BUREAU OF INVESTIGATION
WASHINGTON, D. C.

To: FBI, Memphis   Date: January 20, 1964
Re: Unsub, aka FBI File No. 1
     ELVIS PRESLEY — VICTIM   Lab. No.
     D-440449 IK
     EXTORTION; POSSIBLE THREEAT TO
     PRESIDENT OF THE U. S.

Specimens received 1/17/64

Q1 Post card postmarked "HUNTSVILLE ALA.
JAN 10 1964 5 30 PM" bearing handwritten
address "Presdient Elvis Presly Menphis S,
Tennessee" bearing on reverse side handwritten
note beginning "You Will Be next on my list. . ."
Result of examination:
Specimen Q1 was searched through the appropriate sections of the Anonymous Letter File
without identifying it with any of the writings
therein. A representative copy will be added to
the file for future reference.
Specimen Q1 contains no watermark, indented
writing, or other feature which might assist in
determining its immediate source.
Specimen Q1 is returned herewith. A photograph has been retained.

TO: Director, FBI
FROM: SAC, MEMPHIS (9-NEW)

UNKNOWN SUBJECT, Aka
ELVIS PRESLEY - VICTIM
EXTORTION; POSSIBLE THREAT TO
PRESIDENT OF THE UNITED STATES

Re Memphis teletype to Bureau, 1/15/64.

The following items are enclosed herewith:

Original of post card addressed, "Presdient Elvis Presly Memphis S, tennessee," bearing postmark Huntsville, Ala., Jan. 10, 1964, 5:30 PM.
(2) Two Zerox copies of Item #1.
Enclosed for the Birmingham Division are two Zerox copies of Item #1, described above.
As set forth in referenced teletype, Item #1 was made available to the Memphis Office of the FBI the afternoon of 1/15/64 by Mr. VERNON PRESLEY, Father of ELVIS PRESLEY, movie actor and singer.
Assistant U. S. Attorney C. O. HORTON, Memphis, Tenn., stated he does not consider the contents of the message on the reverse side of the post card to come within the purview of the Federal Extortion Statute.
Item #4 on the post card refers to "JBJ." Since these initials are very close to the initials of the President of the United States, copies of this post card were made available immediately on 1/15/64 to Special Agent in Charge, U. S. Secret Service, Federal Office building, 167 N. Main St.,

Memphis, Tennessee.

As set forth in referenced teletype, UACB, this case is being closed in the Memphis Office with the submission of a confirmatory letter to the U. S. Attorney, Memphis.

L E A D S —

THE BIRMINGHAM DIVISION (INFORMATION)

A copy of this communication is being made available to Birmingham inasmuch as the post card was placed in the U. S. Mails at Huntsville, Ala. And subsequent developments might require investigation in the Birmingham Division.

In late 1970, Elvis Presley declared a wish to tour the FBI headquarters and meet with J. Edgar Hoover. His request was passed up through FBI channels until a briefing memo reached Hoover's desk.
Note the INFORMATION IN BUFILES (Bureau files) paragraph:

Bufiles reflect that Presley has been the victim in a number of extortion attempts which have been referred to the Bureau. Our files also reflect that he is presently involved in a paternity suit pending in Los Angeles, California, and that during the height of his popularity during the latter part of the 1950's and early 1960's his gyrations while performing were the subject of considerable criticism by the public and comment in the press. The files of the Identification Division fail to reflect any arrest record for Presley.

And note the OBSERVATIONS paragraph:

Presley's sincerity and good intentions notwithstanding he is certainly not the type of individual whom the Director would wish to meet. It is noted at the present time he is wearing his hair down to his shoulders and indulges in the wearing of all sorts of exotic dress. A photograph of Presley clipped from today's "Washington Post" is attached and indicated Presley's personal appearance and manner of dress.

J. Edgar Hoover dismissed Presley's request with a curt reply. (Presley had also wanted to become a Special Agent.)
Approximately two years later, President

Richard Nixon felt no qualms about meeting Presley and their picture was taken together in the White House. Presley was given a Federal Narcotics badge. A photograph was taken of the two of them by a White House photographer; a photograph which has become famous — or infamous given the subsequent investigations of the Watergate affair and the resignation of Richard M. Nixon and the later-revealed drug use by Presley.

One letter in the FBI files stamped Feb. 11, 1972, indicates that he ought to receive the same special treatment as Presley received from Nixon:

TO: Mr. Bishop DATE: 12-30-70

FROM: M. A. Jones

SUBJECT: WILLIAM N. MORRIS
        FORMER SHERIFF, SHELBY COUNTY,
        TENNESSEE
        ELVIS PRESLEY
        REQUEST FOR BUREAU TOUR AND MEET
        WITH THE DIRECTOR

Mr. William N. Morris, former Sheriff, Shelby County, Memphis, Tennessee, telephoned Assistant Director Casper from the Washington Hotel today and advised that he was in town with the well-known entertainer Elvis Presley and six other people in Presley's party and inquired concerning the possibility of a tour of our facilities and an opportunity to meet and shake hands with the Director tomorrow, 12-31-70. Morris indicated to Mr. Casper that Presley had just received an award from the President for his work in discouraging the use of narcotics among young people and for his assistance in connection with other youth problems in the Beverly Hills, California, area.

Mr. Casper advised Morris that the Director was out of the city, however, that he, Casper, would see what could be done to arrange a tour for Morris, Presley and party. Morris advised that he could be reached at Room 702, Washington Hotel, telephone number 638-5900.

BACKGROUND:

By memorandum dated 12-22-70, which is

attached, you will recall that Senator George Murphy (Republican-California) telephoned your office on 12-21-70 and advised that Presley had accompanied him, Murphy, to Washington on a flight from Los Angeles and expressed interest in meeting the Director during his stay in Washington.

Murphy described Presley as a very sincere young man who was interested in becoming active in the drive against the use of narcotics, particularly by young people. Murphy indicated that he had arranged an appointment for Presley with John Ingersoll, Director of the Bureau of Narcotics and Dangerous Drugs.

Murphy was advised that the Director was out of the city and not expected to return until around the first of the year at which point he reqthat someone from the Bureau get in touch with Presley and express the Director's regrets. This was done.

M. A. Jones to Mr. Bishop Memo
RE: WILLIAM N. MORRIS AND ELVIS PRESLEY

INFORMATION IN BUFILES:

Bufiles reflect that Presley has been the victim in a number of extortion attempts which have been referred to the Bureau. Our files also reflect that he is presently involved in a paternity suit pending in Los Angeles, California and that during the height of his popularity during the latter part of the 1950's and early 1960's his gyrations while performing were the subject of considerable criticism by the public and comment in the press. The files of the Identification Division fail to reflect any arrest record for Presley.

Our Memphis Office advised that relations with former (??) Morris were excellent during the period he was in office, and that several men from his department were accepted for attendance at the FBI National Academy while he was Sheriff. According to Memphis, Morris is now associated with a public relations firm in that city, but that he has political ambitions and he is anticipated that he will eventually run for Mayor of Memphis.

Our files and the files of the Director's Office fail to reflect that the Director has ever met Presley or Morris.

OBSERVATIONS:

Presley's sincerity and good intentions notwithstanding he is certainly not the type of individual whom the Director would wish to meet. It is noted at the present time he is wearing his hair down to his shoulders and indulges in the wearing of all sorts of exotic dress. A photograph of Presley clipped from today's "Washington Post" is attached and indicates Presley's personal appearance and manner of dress.

RECOMMENDATION:

That the Director permit someone from your office to return former Sheriff Morris' call and advise him that while we will be pleased to afford him, Presley and their party a special tour of our facilities tomorrow, 12-31-70, that it will not be possible for the Director to see them.

January 4, 1971

Mr. Elvis Presley
3764 Highway 51, South
Memphis, Tennessee 38101

Dear Mr. Presley:

I regret that it was not possible for me to see you and your party during your visit to FBI headquarters; however, I do hope you enjoyed your tour of our facilities.

Your generous comments concerning this Bureau and me are appreciated, and you may be sure we will keep in mind your offer to be of assistance.

Sincerely yours,
J. Edgar Hoover

1 - Memphis
1 - Las Vegas
1 - Los Angeles

January 29, 1972

President Richard M. Nixon
1600 Pennsylvania Ave.
Washington, D. C.

Dear Sir,

I had recently read in the newspaper that you had arranged for Elvis Presley, who is a police buff, to receive a Federal Narcotics badge. I too am a police buff, I collect badges and join and support many police associations, besides also being a Special Deputy Sheriff.

I know you can not issue a Federal Narcotics badge to everyone who wants one, but I'm interested whether there are any Federal law enforcement departments that I may be able to be made an Honorary or Associate member, or something of that nature.

I would appreciate any help you or your office may be able to give.

Sincerely,

The "paternity suit" mentioned in the FBI documents resulted in another death threat against Presley when he as appearing in Las Vegas, in August, 1970. There are a very few documents in the FBI files regarding this matter — two are reproduced here.

Abbreviations in the documents are: UNSUB — unknown subject; (PH) — identification done phonetically; S.O. — Sheriff's Office; C.C.S.O. — Clark County Sheriff's Office.

TO   DIRECTOR
        LOS ANGELES
FROM LAS VEGAS (9-300)

SUB: ELVIS PRESLEY - VICTIM EXTORTION.

Re LA tel to director and Las Vegas August twenty eight.

Interviews of Elvis Presley and personnel affiliated with him at Las Vegas, Nevada, have developed no information indicating identity of unsub.

On August twenty six last security officer, International Hotel, Las Vegas, received call from individual identifying self as Jim Reeds (PH) who said he had information that victim was to be kidnapped that night. Caller indicated he had met two men who claimed to have attended party for Presley prior to his trip to Las Vegas. These two men who were not further identified were according to caller setting up plans to kidnap Presley and wanted him to play a part in it. Caller indi-

cated he wanted to alert security personnel and also to advise them that he had no intention of participating in kidnaping. Call believed to have been a long distance call but point of origin unknown.
END PAGE ONE

PAGE TWO
Security personnel of International Hotel, Las Vegas, providing best available security for victim during performances of victim and Clark County S. O. Las Vegas Nevada, has been provided with information relating to this matter. CCSO in contact with hotel security personnel.
Liaison being maintained with and Col. Parker, manager of victim.
END
SLB FBI AWASH DC CLR

August 29, 1970

GENERAL INVESTIGATIVE DIVISION
This is a new manner involving victim, Elvis Presley, well-known entertainer currently appearing at the International Hotel, Las Vegas, Nevada. Anonymous call received by victim's manager at Las Vegas 2:55 P. M., 3/27/70 stating Elvis was going to be kidnapped this weekend. At 6:15 A. M., 8/28/70 wife of a confidante of victim who is with him in Las Vegas, received anonymous call attempting to contact her husband and stated Elvis was going to get it tomorrow night; 45 minutes later same caller again

called and stated a killer, who is a madman, was going to shoot Elvis, that he had a gun with a silencer. Caller said victim had "done him" (killer) wrong about a year ago." Caller requested $50,000 in small bills for information regarding identity of killer whom he knew. Victim involved in paternity suit and victim's attorney believes there may be connection but no facts to substantiate this. Bureau is investigating. Local authorities providing protection to victim's wife and daughter at Los Angeles. Security personnel, International Hotel, Las Vegas, providing protection to victim. Local JCK:mfd authorities, Las Vegas, have been furnished full details.

No further contact or calls made concerning this.

A Lockheed Jetstar airplane, which Elvis Presley owned, but did not use, was the focus of the longest, strangest and most detailed federal investigation in the Presley FBI files.

Apparently Presley knew that the airplane was not making money for him sitting idle; his father, Vernon Presley, had power of attorney to act on behalf of Elvis regarding the aircraft. The investigation, which began about March, 1977, continued even after Presley's death and eventually became a case of Interstate Transportation of Stolen Property — Fraud by Wire.

Essentially, Vernon Presley contracted with Frederick N. P. Pro, of Air Cargo Express (abbreviated ACE), in Miami, Florida. Apparently, the Lockheed Jetstar would be upgraded and refurbished and sold to WWP Leasing, New City via, Air Cargo Express.

For tax purposes (and tax profits), the Jetstar would then be leased back to Presley, then leased again to Air Cargo Express.

All these legal bucket-brigades of back-and-forth leasing and sub-leasing were prime set-ups for fraud.

The key to the government's subsequent action was Frederick N. P. Pro. His checks in payment on the accounts of A. C. E. in Miami were insufficient funds checks.

The following Department of Justice files indicate how convoluted this case became:

UNITED STATES DEPARTMENT OF JUSTICE
FEDERAL BUREAU OF INVESTIGATION

COPY TO: 1 - USA, Memphis
          Attention: AUSA Glen Garland Reid

Report of: SA   Office: Memphis, Tennessee
Date: March 1, 1977

Field Office File #: 87-16994   Bureau File #:

Title: FREDERICK N. P. PRO;
       ELVIS A. PRESLEY - VICTIM

CHARACTER: INTERSTATE TRANSPORTATION OF
STOLEN PROPERTY - FRAUD BY WIRE

Synopsis: VERNON E. PRESLEY, father of
ELVIS A. PRESLEY, entertainer, has power of
attorney to act for his son in business transactions. Acting in this capacity, he entered into a
contract with FREDERICK N. P. PRO, President,
Air Cargo Express, Inc., (ACE), Miami, Florida,
and others, wherein ELVIS A. PRESLEY's plane, a
Lockheed Jetstar, would be sold to WWP Leasing,
New York city. The plane would be upgraded
under FAR 121 Maintenance Program to satisfy
Federal aviation Administration (FAA) requirements. Upgrading of the plane to be supervised
by World Aircraft Exchange (WAC), Boston, Mass.
Plane to then be leased back to PRESLEY and
subleased to ACE. In connection with transactions
AC authorized and WWP approved for payment,
funds spent on the upgrading of the plane in the
amount of $341,500.PRO at the time issued three
checks against the account of ACE on the First
National Bank of Coral Gables, Florida, totaling

$75,510. All PRO's checks were returned by the bank. Subsequently a second similar contract with regard to a second airplane was initiated at which time PRO presented three more checks totaling $95,000, none of which were honored by the bank. ANGELO G. MANNARINO, of AGM Financial Corporation, Miami, Florida, replaced WWP in the second contract, which was nullified through violation of contractual terms. National Bank of Commerce, Memphis, handling PRESLEY's accounts, received telex message from Seven Oak Finance Limited, England, at the request of PRO, reflecting ACE has an account in excess of $500,000. Attorneys for PRESLEY contacted USA, WDT, and investigation to ascertain if FBW exists was instituted.

DETAILS:
Investigation in this case was predicated upon receipt of a request from Assistant United States Attorney GLEN GARLAND REID, advising that he had been contracted by attorneys D. BEECHER SMITH and JAMES N. RAINES of a Memphis law firm who are representing the interests of ELVIS A. PRESLEY. PRESLEY is described by them as a television and motion picture star and entertainer. Mr. REID had reviewed the account presented to him by the attorneys and felt an investigation should be instituted to determine if a violation of the Fraud By Wire Statute did in fact exist.

FEDERAL BUREAU OF INVESTIGATION

Date of transcription 1/18/77

D. BEECHER SMITH, II, was interviewed in the presence of his law associate, FRANK J. GLANKLER, JR., and furnished the following information:

He is employed in the law firm of Montedomico, Heiskell, Davis, Glankler, Brown and Galliland, and maintains his office at 1 Commerce Square, Memphis, Tennessee.

CHARLES H. DAVIS was a senior partner in this law firm and had represented ELVIS A. PRESLEY and the PRESLEY family interests for approximately 21 years. ELVIS PRESLEY maintains a residence at Memphis, Tennessee, and is a popular movie star and entertainer.

Due to the poor health of CHARLES DAVIS, D. BEECHER SMITH became involved in the PRESLEY interests in behalf of the law firm, and in this connection the following facts came to his attention:

ELVIS PRESLEY owned a Lockheed Jetstar airplane, registration number N777KP and manufacturer's serial number 5004.

In June, 1976, there was an outstanding indebtedness on the aircraft in excess of $600,000. This was owed to the American National Bank of Morristown, New Jersey. This particular bank held the mortgage on the plane since it was purchased, according to SMITH, in the general area of this bank.

This aircraft was not being used by PRESLEY in his entertainment business and therefore he as making payments on an asset that was not generating any return on its capital. In addition, attempts to sell the aircraft have resulted in no success.

A meeting was scheduled for June 24, 1976, to arrange a transaction wherein the plane could be refinanced, funds would be provided for its upgrading, and the plane could be leased out and generate a return on the investment of approximately $1,000 per month.

Date reviewed on 1/17/77 of Memphis, Tennessee File # Memphis 87-16994
By SA 67C Date dictated 1/18/77

NIGEL WINFIELD is President of the Commercial Air-Transport Sales, 5553 Northwest 36th Street, Miami, Florida 33166. His telephone is 305-887-1591. WINFIELD had had business dealings in the purchase of airplanes by PRESLEY and therefore was known to him for his capabilities in this field of endeavor. WINFIELD, according to SMITH, introduced VERNON PRESLEY to FREDERICK P. PRO. PRO was identified as the President of Air Cargo Express, Inc., 5533 Northwest 36th Street, Miami, Florida 33166. He has telephone number 305-592-5420. VERNON PRESLEY is the father of ELVIS PRESLEY and, acting with Power of Attorney, assists ELVIS PRESLEY in his business interests.

Present at the meeting on June 24, 1976, were the following individuals:

HANS P. ACHTMANN,
President of W.W.P. Leasing Group,
Suite 856, 230 Park Avenue,
New York city

(212-689-8430);

NIGEL WINFIELD;

FREDERICK P. PRO;

GABRIKL ROBERT CAGGIANO, Attorney,
210 Commercial Street
Boston, Massachusetts
(subsequently determined to be a corporate officer of World Aircraft Exchange, Inc., 1 Court
Street, Boston, Massachusetts);

RAYMOND W. BASZNER
Execution Vice President
World Aircraft Exchange,
1 Court Street, Boston, Massachusetts;

LARRY WOLFSON, Treasurer,
Commercial Air-Transport Sales,
Previously mentioned;

CHARLES H. DAVIS and D. BEECHER SMITH,
Attorneys acting in behalf of ELVIS PRESLEY.

It is SMITH's recollection that WINFIELD, PRO
and CAGGIANO had promoted the idea of a sale-
lease plan involving sub-leasing of the Jetstar
and including an upgrading of the plane.

The transaction contemplated involved the
sale of the Jetstar by ELVIS PRESLEY (through
his father, VRENON PRESLEY acting under Power
of Attorney) to W.W.P. Leasing Group. W.W.P. was
to borrow enough money from the Chemical Bank

of New York to cover both paying off of the present indebtedness on the aircraft, which is over $600,000, and also upgrading this aircraft in order to qualify it for Federal Aviation Regulation 121 Maintenance Program. This upgrading had an estimated cost of $350,000.

Upon completion of the upgrading, the plane allegedly would be valued on the open market at approximately $950,000. With W.W.P. purchasing the plane, the contractual agreement was for ELVIS PRESLEY to lease the plane back for 84 months (7 years) at a monthly rental of $16,755. Thereafter PRESLEY would sub-lease the plane for $17,755 per month for 84 months to Air Cargo Express. This would result in a $1,000 a month profit for PRESLEY, and at the end of the 7-year period PRESLEY had the right to buy back the plane for $1.00. However, the contractual agreement would allow Air Cargo to continue another three years, paying a reduced rental of $10,000 per month.

BASZNER was present at this meeting because he, acting as agent of World Aircraft Exchange, Inc., was supposed to be responsible for supervising the upgrading and modification of the aircraft to qualify it for the Federal Aviation Regulation (FAR) 121 Maintenance Program.

CAGIANO claimed to be representing Air Cargo Express (FRED PRO), according to SMITH, but later told SMITH that he as representing World Aircraft Exchange (BASZNER).

The meeting of June 24, 1976, had to be delayed over into June 25 for the actual signing of the contract. HANS ACHTMANN had to leave on the evening of June 24 and asked CAGGIANO to assist on the following day with the completion of the lease agreement between W.W.P. and ELVIS PRESLEY.

SMITH has no knowledge of any prior association between CAGGIANO and ACHTMANN but feels the request of CAGGIANO was made because of his familiarity with the entire transaction, as well as his abilities as an attorney.

WINFIELD and WOLFSON were present at this meeting because WINFIELD was the aircraft broker and WOLFSON works with him.

SMITH said that the purpose of the meeting on the 24th was not clear to him at its commencement because he had only been called upon by his law associate, CHARLES DAVIS, a few minutes prior to the commencement of the meeting. Due to some changes in the sub-lease agreement, the transaction which originally had been contemplated to be closed in May had been delayed one month.

ACHTMANN had given CAGGIANO a standard form lease consisting of one page, front and back, with approximately 30 short paragraphs and provisions covering the lease agreement for any particular chattel, which in this case was the airplane. CAGGIANO was to complete this lease agreement on June 25, 1976, and return the executed contract to ACHTMANN. The delay in the execution of the contract was due to Mr. DAVIS' poor health and it was to be resumed the following day.

It was on this following day, June 25, 1976, that SMITH learned BASZNER, on behalf of World

Aircraft Exchange, would handle the supervising of the upgrading of the aircraft in order for it to qualify for the FAR 131 Maintenance.

Riders were drafted by Messrs. SMITH, DAVIS, and CAGGIANO, including life insurance, hull insurance, and liabilities.

There were also a provision that the purchase money would be released first to American National Bank to pay off the outstanding indebtedness, then certain funds would go to Air Cargo Express for upgrading the plane, and the balance of the funds were to be released to World Aircraft Exchange for supervising, directing and reporting on the upgrading of the aircraft as statements were issued for services rendered.

On June 23, 1976, the lease agreement was signed by VERNON PRESLEY, acting for ELVIS PRESLEY, and he paid two checks to W.W.P., both in the amount of $16,755, representing the first and 84th monthly rental payments. At the same time FRED PRO wrote three checks to ELVIS PRESLEY, two in the amount of $17,755 each, representing the first and 84th monthly payments, and the third representing a premium for the sub-lease, as required under the sub-lease agreement, in the mount of $40,000. CAGGIANO took his copies of the documents and left; PRO took the keys to the Jetstar and his copies of the documents and left; and PRESLEY took his checks from PRO along with his (PRESLEY's) copies of the documents and left.

However, shortly thereafter it was determined that none of the checks furnished by PRO to PRESLEY were valid and all were returned by the bank.

Later during a telephonic contact with PRO, SMITH was told that the money was coming from Jamaica or some place else and that there had been an error in the transfer of funds.

About a week later, SMITH learned that the Chemical Bank of New York, which was involved in the negotiation of the lease by PRESLEY from W.W.P., reported that the standard chattel lease agreement was unacceptable, and they provided their own draft of the agreement, consisting of approximately 23 pages, to embody the terms of the agreement between ELVIS PRESLEY and W.W.P.

On Tuesday, July 13, 1976, SIDNEY ZNEIMER, an attorney for W.W.P., came to Memphis with the document, and certain changes were made with the approval of ZNEIMER as spokesman for W.W.P. and the Chemical Bank of New York. While ZNEIMER was in the law office with SMITH and DAVIS, CAGGIANO and BASZNER arrived unannounced. BASZNER had certain invoices for payment for upgrading on the aircraft. DAVIS did not want VERNON PRESLEY to sign them as BASZNER desired, because under the original rider of the lease, the release of funds for upgrading was the responsibility of W.W.P. PRESLEY then, with the approval of the attorneys, signed these invoices evidencing approval that W.W.P. make the payments as it was not desired that PRESLEY be placed in a position of supervising the upgrading and modification of the airplane.

The invoices were dated July 7, 1976, on stationery of World Aircraft Exchange, Inc., and are as follows:

WORLD AIRCRAFT EXCHANGE INC.

Executive Offices:
One Court Street
Boston, Mass. 02105
U.S.A.
(617) 227-3155

Statement 106 E.P.
July 7, 1976

W.W.P. Leasing Corp.
230 Park Avenue
New York, New York

Per Lease Amendment Document between W.W.P. Leasing Corp. and Elvis A. Presley, this statement will serve to authorize a disbursement of funds in the amount specified below to the following party:

Amount: $17,500.00
Payee: Frederick P. Pro, President, Air Cargo Express Inc.
For: Certification for F.A.A. 121 per Agreement, Operational Setup and Flight Management

Approved for payment by
W. W. P. Leasing Corp.

Elvis A. Presley
By:
Per Power of Attorney

WORLD AIRCRAFT EXCHANGE INC.

Executive Offices:
One Court Street
Boston, Mass. 02105
U.S.A.
(617) 227-3155

Statement 206 E.P.
July 7, 1976

W.W.P. Leasing Corp.
230 Park Avenue
New York, New York

Per Lease Amendment Document between W.W.P.
Leasing Corp. and Elvis A. Presley, this statement
authorizes the disbursement of funds, in the
amount specified below, to the following party:

Amount: $32,000.00
Payee: Air Cargo Express Inc. and Dallas
Airmotive
For: Purchase of Part 121 Avionics Equipment
       Flight Data Recorder
       Cockpit Voice Recorder
       Ground Proximity Warning Indicator
       Part 121 Checks

Approved for payment by
W. W. P. Leasing Corp.

Elvis A. Presley
By: (Vernon E. Presley)

Per Power of Attorney

WORLD AIRCRAFT EXCHANGE INC.

Executive Offices:
One Court Street
Boston, Mass. 02105
U.S.A.
227-3155

Statement 306 E.P.
July 7, 1976

W.W.P. Leasing Corp.
230 Park Avenue
New York, New York

Per Lease Amendment Document between W.W.P. Leasing Corp. and Elvis A. Presley, this statement authorizes the disbursement of funds, in the amount specified below to the following party:

Amount: $129,500.00
Payee: Trans World Industries Inc.
For: Part 121 Maintenance Systems,
Certification and Modification,
Cardex System

Approved for payment by
W. W. P. Leasing Corp.

Elvis A. Presley
By: (Vernon E. Presley)

Per Power of Attorney

WORLD AIRCRAFT EXCHANGE INC.

Executive Offices:
One Court Street
Boston, Mass. 02105
U.S.A.
227-3155

Statement 406 E.P.
July 7, 1976

W.W.P. Leasing Corp.
230 Park Avenue
New York, New York

Per Lease Amendment Document between W.W.P. Leasing Corp. and Elvis A. Presley, this statement authorizes the disbursement of funds, in the amount specified below, to the following party:

Amount: $45,000.00
Payee: World Aircraft Exchange Inc.
For: Part 121 Certification and Aircraft Modification and Update Program

Approved for payment by
W. W. P. Leasing Corp.

Elvis A. Presley
By: (Vernon E. Presley)
Per Power of Attorney

WORLD AIRCRAFT EXCHANGE INC.

Executive Offices:
One Court Street
Boston, Mass. 02105
U.S.A.
227-3155

Statement 506 E.P.
July 7, 1976

W.W.P. Leasing Corp.
230 Park Avenue
New York, New York

Per Lease Amendment Document between W.W.P.
Leasing Corp. and Elvis A. Presley, this statement
will authorize the disbursement of funds, in the
amount specified below, to the following party:

Amount: $117,500.00
Payee: Frederick P. Pro, President, Air Cargo
Express Inc.
For: Port 121 Inspection and Operational Flight
Proving Tests and Aircraft Improvement Program,
i.e. Purchase of Service Bulletin 230, A - E.

Approved for payment by
W. W. P. Leasing Corp.

Elvis A. Presley
By: (Vernon E. Presley)
Per Power of Attorney

During this same meeting on July 13, 1975, the addendum to the lease entitled "Rider No. 1" was retyped and again stated that the responsibility for supervising the modification and upgrading of the aircraft was that of World Aircraft Exchange, Inc., for which World Aircraft Exchange, Inc., was to be paid. At the conclusion of the meeting, ZNEIMER took the new lease and the two-page rider signed by VERNON PRESLEY back to New York City.

At this point SMITH's attention was drawn to the upper right-hand corner of the five statements referred to above, and he was questioned concerning the words "Statement 106 E.P." The numbers 206, 3067, 406 and 506 were each entered on the other four invoices which totaled $341,500. SMITH was unable to explain this and felt that World Aircraft should be able to clarify this matter.

On July 20, 1976, SMITH was called to DAVIS' home and was presented with a poorly drafted two-page document providing for an assignment by Air Cargo of its sub-lease to a company called A.G.M. Financial Corporation. DAVIS had received this in the mail from FRED P. PRO. SMITH had learned that PRO claimed he could not do business with ACHTMANN as W.W.P. was too hard-nosed. PRO wanted the original lease with W.W.P. to be altered and replace W.W.P. with A.G.M. Financial. This conceivably would cause a change from the chemical Bank of New York to another bank.

To SMITH's recollection, prior to the signing of the lease contract on July 13, 1976, there was a meeting of CAGGIANO with VERNON PRESLEY. DAVIS and SMITH were present and CAGGIANO had gone to tell PRESLEY of PRO's problems with ACHTMANN. CAGGIANO was interested in replacing W.W.P. due to their slow funding and disbursement of money. Unannounced, NIGKL WINFIELD arrived at the meeting from Miami, and the discussion continued to the point that DAVIS asked who would be recommended to replace W.W.P. in the lease. As SMITH recall, WINFIELD said in slow words, "A.G.M. Financial." This request was denied on behalf of PRESLEY.

SMITH then returned to his aforementioned meeting with DAVIS at DAVIS' house and the two-page assignment. VERNON PRESLEY arrived at the house and advised them that CAGGIANO had flown to Memphis on Thursday after the Tuesday on which the revised lease agreement had been executed.

CAGGIANO brought with him a cashier's check in the approximate amount of $338,000 from the Chemical Bank of New York. PRESLEY also told him that ACHTMANN of W.W.P. had called him previously and requested that instead of W.W.P. disbursing the funds, as provided under the rider of the revised lease, PRESLEY should disburse the funds for the upgrading of the plane.

ACHTMANN said he did not know whether the work was done or not and did not want the responsibility. SMITH commented that ACHTMANN was in the aircraft leasing business and should have no problem understanding whether the work had been completed or not and he could not understand ACHTMANN's position acting for

W.W.P. in this latest development. PRESLEY further informed them that CAGGIANO, BASZNER and PRO had been to Memphis and contacted PRESLEY directly. They went to the Whitehaven branch of the National Bank of Commerce and in the presence of CLARENCE CARTER, the bank official, PRESLEY accepted their invoices and drafted one personal check to FREDERICK PRO in the amount of $17,500, with the notation on the check "Ref 106 E.P." SMITH had in his possession a copy of this check bearing the endorsement FREDERICK P. PRO.

PRESLEY also had prepared four cashier's checks payable to those corporations designated on the invoices prepared on World Aircraft Exchange stationery. These checks would have been $32,000 to Air Cargo Express, Inc., and Dallas Airmotive, $129,500 to Trans World Industries, and $45,000 to World Aircraft Exchange, Inc.

The invoice in the mount of $117,500 payable to FREDERICK P. PRO, President, Air Cargo Express, Inc., was not satisfied in its entirety. PRESLEY deducted $78,510 representing the checks which PRO had originally given and subsequently were returned by the bank. This resulted in a net of $38,990 given to PRO at this time.

It is SMITH's opinion that ACHTMANN and W.W.P. were either operating in conjunction with CAGGIANO, BASZNER, PRO and their related corporations, or at least they dealt directly with PRESLEY and in the absence of PRESLEY's attorneys effecting a change in the contract for the disbursement of funds. SMITH believes that he was told by DAVIS that ACHTMANN had told DAVIS that he requested PRESLEY pay the monies directly to these people.

The first monthly rental payment was not due from Air Cargo Express until August 25, 1976. However, Air Cargo Express indicated an interest in another aircraft belonging to ELVIS PRESLEY and an arrangement was again proposed by the broker, NIGEL WINFIELD. This arrangement was being proposed in behalf of A.G.M. Financial Corporation, which is the same organization previously submitted by Pro to replace W.W.P. in the first contract. This corporation was formed by one ANGELO G. MANNARINO, with a business address of 14423 Southwest 74th Avenue, Miami, Florida (305-251-7209). A.G.M. sought to fill the same role accomplished by W.W.P. with regard to the Jetstar on another plane of PRESLEY's, a Dassult-Falcon, Model Number 20-C, Serial Number 30. Agreements were drafted between A.GG.W. and ELVIS PRESLEY, which were executed on July 30, 1976. A similar type sale and lease back arrangement was entered into as previously described at the initial stages of this interview. VERNON PRESLEY gave personal checks to ANGELO MANNARINO in the approximate amount of $53,000, which MANNARINO subsequently cashed. PRO presented PRESLEY with three more checks totaling approximately $95,000, again representing the first and 84th monthly payments under the sub-lease and a check for $40,000 premium for the lease. Again none of PRO's checks were honored by the bank.

Because MANNARINO and A.G.M. could not

secure funding for the sale-lease back arrangement on the Falcon, PRESLEY was able to call off this deal. However, A.G.M. still wrongfully retains $50,000 paid it as a deposit.

During the negotiations for the second sale-lease back agreement, Air Cargo Express did not tender its second monthly rental payment. Numerous telephone calls followed checking up on the progress and upgrading of the plane, and PRO told SMITH that the delay in funding by the Chemical Bank had caused his company to be somewhat behind in achieving 121 Maintenance. PRO asked for and did receive an extension, granted him by W.W.P.

Over the next few weeks PRO made various representations to PRESLEY and SMITH concerning the 121 Maintenance Program, including such things as the wings of the Jetstar and been removed and X-rayed for any faults and that tests had been run on the plane. PRO also stated that at different times he had flown the plane on tests with various FAA officials, and it would be just a matter of days before the 121 certificate would be granted by FAA.

A notice of default was mailed to Air Cargo demanding immediate payment or else repossession of the plane, and on October 11, 1976, the following communication was received:

EXHIBIT F

VIA WUI+

N B C MFS

896126 CIDCO G

11.19.76

HERE IS SEVEN OAK FINANCE LTD

ENGLAND

TO   NATIONAL BANK OF COMMERCE
       4696 ELVIS PRESLEY BOULEVARD
       MENTHIS
       TENNESSE

FOR THE ATTENTION OF CLARENCE CARTER
WHITEHAVEN BRANCH TLX NO. 533178

WITH REGARDS TO ELVIS PRESLEY AIR CARGO
EXPRESS TRANSACTION, BY THE REQUEST OF
MR FREDERICK PRO, SEVEN OAK FINANCE LTD
HAS BANK CONFIRMATION THAT AIR CARGO
EXPRESS HAS AN ACCOUNT IN EXCESS OF
500,000 US DOLLARS
REGARDS

A C SCOTT-BROWN
SEVEN OAK FINANCE LTD
TIME HERE 12.55 SM

Although this wire was received, no payments
were received from Air Cargo Express and ultimately one of ELVIS PRESLEY's pilots went to
Miami to retake the plane. Upon its return to
Memphis, its log book was reviewed and revealed
that none of the funds in excess of a quarter of

a million dollars which had been paid out upgrading and modifying the plane to qualify it for 121 Maintenance had been applied to the plane.

SMITH summarized by saying that PRO, through various corporations under his control, obtained over $200,000 from PRESLEY by representing these funds would be used to upgrade the aircraft to qualify it for 121 Maintenance. PRO also sent various checks which were subsequently dishonored by the banks on which they were drawn.

Over $40,000 was paid to BASZNER of World Aircraft Exchange for work to be performed on the aircraft, which was not accomplished. SMITH has since been told that PRO has left the country for England and the Air Cargo Express office in Miami is not in operation.

In addition, referring to notes maintained by his associate, FRANK J. GLANKLER, JR., it was determined that BASZNER had been called on November 3, 1976, by telephone. The answering party advised that he was not there but that ROBERT CIAGGIANO was available. This was the first indication, November 3, 1976, that CAGGIANO was an official of World Aircraft Exchange. SMITH believes he is the President of the corporation. BASZNER, according to the notes, called Memphis back and allegedly claimed that W.W.P. would withhold disbursements until such times as the individual work was done. PRO had spoken to PRESLEY, according to BASZNER, and was getting the plane fireproofed, ?? and re-establishing its crash worthiness. BASZNER, who had arranged for the purchase of the plane, received a commission for this, but PRO had told him that a voice recorder and other equipment were being provided for the plane. BASZNER received about $45,000 to provide the financing and technical program and was following up the certification of the plane and would verify its appraisal. Allegedly BASZNER had five checks from Pro, all of which were bad.

SMITH said that W.W.P. had been located by CAGGIANO to set up the financing in this first transaction with PRESLEY. WINFIELD of Commercial Air Transport voices the same claim. W.W.P. was to get two months rent as a commission and then receive no further reimbursements. W.W.P. was the lessor and owner of the plane, the Jetstar, and the lease was assigned to the Chemical Bank of New York. THOMAS MICHELS, 55 Water Street, Suite 1822, New York City, was the bank official involved.

SMITH further stated that he had been informed by RICHARD R. NEVILLE, Chief, Federal Aviation Administration, Miami, Florida, that on September 7, 1976, Span East Airlines, Inc., doing business as Air Cargo Express, requested that the FAA hold operating certificate CE-24(C) until such time as the company could again comply with the requirements of the Federal Aviation regulations. The carrier also voluntarily surrendered its operating certificate on September 7, 1976, which was cancelled the same date.

SMITH believes that he has had conversations with PRO subsequent to that September 7 date, wherein PRO informed him of additional repairs progressing on the Jetstar. SMITH is endeavoring to locate his office records to substantiate these conversations.

As a matter of information SMITH furnished a copy of the Aircraft Lease Agreement between ELVIS PRESLEY and Air Cargo Express, Inc., dated in May, 1976. This was superseded by the contract ultimately signed July 13, 1976. Contained in the May, 1976, proposed contract was a clause which would allow payments to be paid directly to the First Trust Company of Houston, 811 Rusk Avenue, Houston. SMITH was unable to explain why this particular bank was designated and is not familiar with who drew up this contract.

Contained in Clause 13 was indication that Air Cargo Express, Inc., was located at 1750 Northwest 69th Avenue, Miami, Florida.

PRO also furnished a document by Span Air, Inc., FREDEREICK P. PRO, President, certifying this to be a public corporation listed with the Securities and Exchange Commission.

SMITH was unaware of the relationship of Span Air, Inc., with Air Cargo Express.

A Provision to the Lease dated July 15, 1976, and identified as Rider No. 1, was furnished by HANS ACHTMANN to VERNON PRESLEY and related, in part, to the release of funds from W.W.P. The second paragraph is as follows: "The Balance of the payment between American National Bank and the capitalized cost of Nine Hundred Fifty Thousand Dollars ($950,000.00) shall be paid to Elvis A. Presley, who will distribute such funds for the purpose of up-dating said Aircraft to comply with F.A.R. 121 specifications and 121 Maintenance Program." Although this rider was initialed by ACHTMANN, it was contrary to the original lease agreement which would put the burden on Air Cargo Express and World Aircraft Exchange, Inc.

SMITH questioned the purpose for ACHT-MANN doing this because it appeared that ACHT-MANN felt he was being put in the middle between PRESLEY and PRO. If PRO or his associates were doing something irregular with regard to the repairs to the plane, and reports of repairs to W.W.P. caused payments to be made to World Aircraft in error, ACHTMANN would be responsible to a degree.

SMITH also had in his possession a copy of "Minutes of a Special Meeting of the Board of Directors of Air Cargo Express, Inc." This is dated June 30, 1976, and identified the directors as being FRED PRO, President, and ROY SMITH acting as secretary. According to the minutes, a discussion was held as to who should be authorized to sign and execute instruments of purchase of the aircraft in behalf of the corporation. A resolution was made and passed that FREDERICK P. PRO, President, be authorized to sign and execute lease and sub-lease of the aircraft from ELVIS A. PRESLEY. These minutes are signed FREDERICK P. PRO, Chairman; ROY E. SMITH, Secretary.

D. BEECHER SMITH, Attorney, 1 Commerce Square, Memphis, Tennessee, advised that he had been in receipt of a Dun and Bradstreet report relative to Air Cargo Express, Inc., with a business address of 1750 Northwest 69th Avenue, Miami. The report reflects the company was started in 1976 with 10 employees and on April 15, 1976, FREDERICK PRO, President, deferred financial information. The officers were identified as FREDERICK PRO, President; CHESTER HORTON, Secretary and Treasurer; and RAY SMITH, Vice President. He business was incorporated in Florida in January, 1976.

PRO, born in 1926, is divorced. His background, according to the report, is that he graduated from Temple University, obtaining a degree in Industrial Engineering and a Master's degree in Electronic Engineering. After military service, he was with RCA until 1958, was Vice President and General Manager of Budd Electronics during 1963, and in 1970 he was Vice President for the Railway Division of Budd Company. He spearheaded the Metroliner (New York City, Washington, D. C.) Trailing Program. He also received the 1964 Paris LeBourget Air Award for New Concepts. He also served as consultant to a governmental agency for Futuristic Electronic Transportation Exploitations. In 1972, as Investor and Chairman of the Board of Parker West Corporation, Boynton Beach, Florida, he set up this as a holding company owned by local and foreign investors. IN rapid succession, Parker West Corporation purchased the assets of Glassic Industries, Inc., changed the name to Glassic Motors, Inc., manufacturing antique replicas, and he purchased assets of Electronic Systems Division of Dynamics Corporation of America, which he changed to Rel-Reeves, Inc. This organization manufactured record retrieval equipment.

He set up Romulus Motor Car Company, Inc.,

manufacturing automobile replicas. He set up Interpole Communications, Inc., Precision Electronics Corporation, and Glassic Marketing, Inc., which soon merged into one or another of the above outlined corporations. On July 22, 1975, Parker West Corporation and its three subsidiaries, Glassic Motors, Inc., Rel-Reeves, Inc., and Romulus Motor Car Company, Inc., filed voluntary petition for arrangement under Chapter XI, U. S. District Court, Miami. This is isted under case # 75-999. Total liabilities were reported at $9,143,000, and total assets of $16,417,000. Attorneys were identified as Maas, Rogers, and Chauncey, 321 Royal Poinciana Plaza, Palm Beach, Florida. Referee was PAUL HYMAN, and filing at the same time was FREDERICK P. PRO under case # 75-1005.

Information concerning RAY SMITH or CHESTER HORTON was undetermined by Dun and Bradstreet.

Air Cargo Express is affiliated through FREDERICK PRO with Worldwide Communications, Inc., incorporated in Florida in 1976 and located at the same address as a holding company. Trident National Corporation, Inc., incorporated in Florida in 1975 or 1976 as an air cargo organization, is another affiliate, as is Span Air, Inc., purchased March 10, 1976, as a freight transport organization. Dun and Bradstreet reported that Air Cargo Express moved from 5757 Northwest 27th Avenue, Miami, Florida, (305-883-5533) to 5553 Northwest 36th Street, Miami, Florida.

On August 10, 1976, according to Dun and

Bradstreet, the local press reported a suit in the amount of $1,289 was entered against Air Cargo Express, Inc., by State Southern Management Company, Inc., in County Court, Miami, under docket # 7612697 SP-OS.

On February 14, 1977, D. BEECHER SMITH, attorney, telephonically advised that the pilot for ELVIS PRESLEY who would have knowledge of the condition of the plane before and after it was surrendered to FRED PRO, as MILO HIGH,

VERNON PRESLEY can be contacted at the Graceland Estates and an appointment arranged by calling him on the private line

SMITH also advised that he has received a call from ANGELO G. MANNARINO who was in Miami. MANNARINO told him that PRO had sent "two goons" to MANNARINO to force him to make a $70,000 loan to PRO.

SMITH also had a copy of Minutes of a meeting of the Board of Directors of Air Cargo Express, Inc., which reads as follows:

MINUTES OF A SPECIAL MEETING OF THE BOARD OF DIRECTORS OF AIR CARGO EXPRESS INC.

A special meeting of the Board of Directors of Air cargo express Inc., was held at <u>5553 N.W. 36<u>th</u></u> <u>Street</u> Miami, Florida on <u>June 20</u>, 1976, at 10:00 a.m., pursuant to waiver of written notice.

All of the Directors being present, <u>Fred Pro, President</u> (title), acted as Chairman, and <u>Roy Smith</u> acted as secretary.

A discussion was held as to who should be authorized to sign and execute instruments of purchase of aircraft in behalf of the corporation. Upon a motion duly made, seconded and carried, the following resolution was passed:

BE IT RESOLVED that Frederick P. Pro, President be authorized to sign and execute Lease and Sub-Leases of Aircraft from Elvis A. Presley.

Therebeing no further business the meeting was adjourned.

Dated this 20 day of June, 1976.

Chairman

Secretary

On February 18, 1977, this case was discussed with Assistant United States Attorney GLEN GARLAND REID at which time he agreed to issue grand jury subpoenas for

The possibility exists of not only a Fraud By Wire violation, but a conspiracy to promote same. *This August 8, 1977 FBI document summaries the Jetstar aircraft case to that date:*

UNITED STATES DEPARTMENT OF JUSTICE
FEDERAL BUREAU OF INVESTIGATION

1 - Fraud Section, Criminal Division, U.S. Department of Justice (Attn: BOB HICKEY) (Enc. 1)
Copy to: 1 - Chicago Strike Force (Attn: GARY SHAPIRO) (Enc. 1)
1 - Cleveland Strike Force (Attn: M. MICHAELSON)
1 - U.S. Attorney, Southern District of New York

(ATTN: MIKE CAREY)
Report of: Office: INDIANAPOLIS
Date: August 8, 1977

Field Office File #: 87-227204

Title: OPFOPEN
(OO: INDIANAPOLIS)

FREDERICK N. P. PROP
ELVIS A. PRESLEY - VICTIM
Character: INTERSTATE TRANSPORTATION OF
STOLEN PROPERTY - FRAUD BY WIRE; TOP
THIEF PROGRAM

Synopsis: VERNON E. PRESLEY, father of
ELVIS A. PRESLEY, entertainer, has power of
attorney to act for his son in business transac-
tions. He entered into a contract with FREDER-
ICK N. P. PRO, President, Air Cargo Express, Inc.,
(ACE), Miami, Florida, and others wherein
PRESLEY's plane, a Lockheed Jetstar, would be
sold to WWP Leasing Company, New York City.
The plane would be up-graded under FAR 121
Maintenance Program to satisfy Federal Aviation
Administration (FAA) requirements. This up-
grading would be supervised by World Aircraft
Exchange (WAE), Boston, and the plane then
leased back to PRESLEY and sub-leased to ACE.
In connection with this, WAE authorized and
WWP approved for payment funds spent on the
up-grading of the plane in the amount of
$341,500. PRO at the time issued three checks
against the account of ACE on the First National

Bank of Coral Gables, Florida, totaling $75,510. All PRO's checks were returned by the bank. Subsequently, a second similar contract with regard to a second airplane of PRESLEY's was initiated and PRO presented three more checks totaling $95,000, none of which were honored by the bank. ANGELO G. MANNARINO of AGM Financial Corporation, Miami, Florida, replaced WWP in the second contract which was nullified through violation of contractual terms. National Bank of Commerce, Memphis, handling PRESLEY's accounts received Telex message from Seven Oak Finance Limited, England, at the request of PRO reflecting ACE has an account in excess of $500,000. Attorney for PRESLEY made available copy of "Wall Street Journal" describing "offshore" bank operations including Mercantile Bank and Trust Company, Kingston, British West Indies. PRO was given checks totaling $167,000 by PRESLEY for work and tests involving PRESLEY's plane which work has subsequently been determined was never performed. PRESLEY also gave MANNARINO a check for $55,830.35 on the second contract. PRO told PRESLEY he was going to England to get the money and return it to Memphis claiming "something like one half million dollars." FAA officials have no documents filed by PRO for the Lockheed Jetstar. Dallas Airmotive never performed work attributed to it as set forth on invoices relative to PRESLEY's plane.

ENCLOSURES:
Enclosed for Fraud Section, Criminal Division,

U.S. Department of Justice; Chicago, Illinois, Strike Force; Cleveland, Ohio, Strike Force; and U.S. Attorney, Southern District of New York, one copy each of Memphis report of SA dated August 2, 1977.

DETAILS:

Investigation in this case was predicated upon a request received from the United States Attorney's Office (USA), Western District of Tennessee, Memphis, Tennessee, wherein they had been contacted by attorneys for ELVIS A. PRESLEY, an entertainer, indicating they felt a violation of Federal law had taken place. They identified the principal as FREDERICK N. P. PRO and their client, PRESLEY, as the victim losing in excess of $400,000.

PRESLEY owned a Lockheed Jetstar airplane which had an outstanding indebtedness of over $600,000 as of June, 1976. This plane was not being used by PRESLEY in his entertainment business and he therefore was making payments on an asset that was not generating any return on its capital. In addition, attempts to sell the aircraft had resulted in no success.

In June, 1976, a meeting was arranged which included the following people:

HANS ACHTMANN, President, WWP Leasing Group, New York City.

NIGEL WINFIELD, President, and LARRY WOLFSON, Treasurer, Commercial Air Transport Sales, Miami, Florida.

FREDERICK P. PRO, President, Air Cargo Express, Inc., Miami, Florida.

GABRIEL ROBERT CAGGIANO, Attorney and Corporate Officer, World Aircraft Exchange, Boston, Massachusetts.

RAYMOND W. BASZNER, Vice President, World Aircraft Exchange, Boston, Massachusetts.

D. BEECHER SMITH and CHARLES H. DAVIS, Attorneys for ELVIS PRESLEY, Memphis, Tennessee.

WINFIELD, PRO and CAGGIANO had promoted the idea of a sale-lease program involving the sub-leasing of the Jetstar and including an up-grading of the plane. The transaction would be the sale of PRESLEY's Jetstar to WWP Leasing Group. WWP in turn would borrow enough money from the Chemical Bank of New York to cover both the paying off of the present indebtedness on the aircraft, over $600,000, and also upgrading this aircraft in order to qualify it for Federal Aviation Regulation (FAR) 121 Maintenance Program. This up-grading had an estimated cost of $350,000.

Upon completion of the up-grading, the plane allegedly would be valued on the open market at approximately $950,000. With WWP purchasing this plane, the contractual agreement would continue in that PRESLEY would then lease the plane back for 84 months at a monthly rental of $16,755 and he in turn would sub-lease the plane for $17,755 per month for 84 months to Air Cargo Express (ACE). This way PRESLEY would profit by $1,000 a month and, at the end of the seven year period, he had the right to buy back the plane for $1.00. However, the agreement would allow ACE to continue another three years paying a reduced rental of $10,000 per month.

BASZNER, who was at the meeting held on June 24, 1976, was an agent for World Aircraft Exchange, Inc., and was supposed to be responsible for supervising the up-gradings and modifications of the aircraft to qualify for the FAR 121 Maintenance Program.

When the contract was signed on June 25, 1976, VERNON PRESLEY, acting for ELVIS PRESLEY, paid two checks to WWP both in the amount of $16,755 representing the first and eighty-fourth monthly rental payments. PRO wrote three checks to ELVIS PRESLEY, two in the amount of $17,755 each representing the first and eighty-fourth monthly payments, and the third check in the amount of $40,000 representing a premium for the sub-lease. All three checks of PRO, on the Flagship, First National Bank of Coral Gables, Coral Gables, Florida, were

Through contact with of Dallas Airmotive, which subsequently was named Cooper Airmotive, it was determined that ACE, Span East Airlines, WWP Leasing Corporation and World Aircraft Exchange, Inc., had never had a file or account number with the company. No equipment was ordered or obtained from Dallas Airmotive by PRO or any of his representatives.

Special Agents and Federal Bureau of Investigation, met with Special Agent Federal Bureau of Investigation, at 10:00 PM Park West, New York city, New York. And are registered in Room 311 of the same hotel where they are lodged with PHILLIP KARL KITZNER, JR. and furnished the following information concerning information they had obtained during the time they had been with KITZER:

And KITZER departed Miami, Florida aboard National Airlines Flight 90 at approximately 6:30 PM on May 5, 1977. None of the three individuals sat together and thus there was no discussion aboard this flight regarding activities of KITZER. All three individuals arrived at the Laguardia Airport in New York City at approximately 9:00 PM on May 5, 1977, and thereafter registered at the Mayflower Hotel.

After the meeting with was concluded, KITZER telephonically contacted FRED PRO to set up a meeting for May 6, 1977. This telephone call was made from the Mayflower Hotel in KITZER's room. PRO met with KITZER, and at the Essex House Hotel near the Mayflower Hotel at approximately 4:20 PM or 4:30 PM through a period of time slightly before 6:00 PM on May 6, 1977. While going to meet with PRO, KITZER advised and that was a good guy to know and if KITZER who would in turn contact and schedule a sit-down conference in New York to iron out any problems.

A business card provided to and by PRO indicated his full name as FREDERICK P. PRO and he was shown as the director, United States of America, of Trident Consortium located at 128 Central Park South, New York, Telex Number 12041, telephone number 212-757-8037. PRO was described as a white male, approximately 6'1" in height, weighting 190 to 200 pounds. He has graying hair and wears glasses. His build is heavy, and he is approximately 45 to 50 years of age. PRO alleges that he is an Italian.

KITZER has indicated that PRO is not the true name of the above individual.

Upon initially meeting PRO, PRO inquired of KITZER as to whether it was okay to talk in front of and to which KITZER replied that it was all right. Thereafter, the following took place:

PRO indicated that at the present time he handles approximately 150 telephone calls per day arranging deals produced by eleven individuals working as brokers for him through the United States. He indicates that he works from approximately 8:00 AM through 12:00 Midnight each day.

At the present time, PRO indicated he was operating Trident Consortium in New York City. PRO stated that the company appears to operate worldwide with PRO acting as the U. S. agent. PRO stated, however, that he owns and controls the whole corporation. PRO indicated that he intends to open branches in other countries and that with this arrangement, it would be easy to confirm various financial instruments via telex from foreign countries.

In this part of the FBI document, Frederick Pro admits he planned to con Presley out of the Jetstar aircraft — Pro's colleague Phillip Kitzer had indicated he thought it was (a) "mission impossible." Pro replied that he had shown Kitzer exactly what a "mission impossible" was because he had, in fact, obtained the aircraft. And he had told Kitzer he had the aircraft from the aircraft's air-to-ground telephone system while in flight.

PRO stated that he conned ELVIS PRESLEY out of PRESLEY's Tri-Star aircraft. KITZER advised PRO that PRO had previously told him that he was going to get PRESLEY's aircraft and that KITZER had told PRO that was "mission impossible." PRO replied back that he had shown KITZER what "mission impossible was and asked KITZER if he recalled that PRO had telephonically contacted him shortly after obtaining PRESLEY's aircraft. PRO indicated that immediately after leaving the ground in Memphis, Tennessee with PRESLEY's aircraft he used the aircraft's air-to-ground telephone system to call KITZER and tell him at his home in Minnesota that he had acquired the airplane.

After acquiring PRESLEY's aircraft, PRO then contacted either the First National City Bank of New York or the Chase Manhattan Bank in New York and obtained a $1,000,000 mortgage on the aircraft. When the first payment came due, PRO indicated he skated with the proceeds and left the bank holding the aircraft. PRO stated that he told the bank they had bought themselves a plane. PRO indicated he had also given PRESLEY other paper but it was not specified what this was.

In regard to aircraft transactions, PRO indicated that he preferred to accept aircraft from individuals who desired to have their aircraft repaired. Instead of repairing the aircraft, PRO indicted he disassembled the aircraft and sold the parts.

According to PRO, his usual method of busting out a company is to take viable company assets which include both liquid and semi-liquid assets and to convert them to less valuable assets which only appear to be valuable. He diverts cash flow and increases business expenses until bankruptcy gradually occurs. In short, he swaps viable assets for less viable ones.

Here (8/26/77) Elvis Presley is identified as VICTIM (DECEASED):

TO: DIRECTOR, FBI (87-143601)

FROM: LEGAT, LONDON (87-547) (RDC)

SUBJECT: FREDEREICK W. P. PRO;
        ELVIS A. PRESLEY - VICTIM (DECEASED)
        ITSP; FBW
        OO: MEMPHIS

Kitzer and others in this con game are arrested, but Frederick Pro, who had posted bond in the case, is now a fugitive:

MM0765 2922300Z
RR HQ BS IP LS ME NY
DE MM
R 192300Z OCT 77
FM MIAMI P
TO DIRECTOR (57-143601) ROUTINE
BOSTON (57-18320) ROUTINE
INDIANAPOLIS *57-22 72 0) ROUTINE
LOUISVILLE ROUTINE
MEMPHIS (27-102974) ROUTINE
NEW YORK (87-79558) ROUTINE
ET
E F T O
OPFOPEN, TIP, OZ: INDIANAPOLIS, MIAMI FILE 87-39331.
FREDERICK W. P. PRO - FUGITIVE; ET AL, ITSP; FBW, MF; CONSPIRACY, 83: MEMPHIS, MIAMI FILE 196-68.
FOR INFORMATION OF RECEIVING OFFICES, ON OCTOBER 19, 1977, PHILLIP KARL KITZER WAS PRESENTED BEFORE. U.S. MAGISTRATE CHARLENE M. SORRENTINO AT MIAMI, FLORIDA, FOR IDENTITY HEARING. KITZER WAS REMANDED TO CUSTODY OF U. S. MARSHAL, MIAMI, FLORIDA, UNTIL OCTOBER 21, 1977, OR SCHEDULED BOND HEARING.

TWO MM 87-39331 AND MM 196-6B E F T O

Laurence Wolfson appeared before U. S. Magistrate Sorrentino, Supra, on October 19, 1977. Wolfson was represented at his identity hearing by an individual who is not his regular attorney, Louis Williams. Wolfson instructed by magistrate to inform her office by Friday, October 21, 1977, whether or not Williams would represent him (Wolfson or else appear before U. S. magistrate at that time for the appointment of counsel. Wolfson's removal hearing scheduled for November 3, 1977. Wolfson had previously posted bond on October 18, 1977, subsequent to his arrest.

Attempts to arrest Raymond W. Baszner at his residence, 16398 Stone Haven Road, Miami Lakes, Florida, early a.m. October 19, 1977, unsuccessful.

Baszner's employer, was contacted; and we advised he would have Baszner appear at Miami FBI office at 9 a.m., October 26, 1977.

The following descriptive data was obtained from Baszner: sex male, race white, date of birth March 11, 1944, Social Security account number height 6'1", weight 250 pounds, hair brown, eyes blue.

ET

October 18, 1977: Frederick Pro Is arrested in New York City, but "UPON ADVICE OF COUNSEL, DECLINED TO DISCUSS SUBSTANTIVE CHARGES."

NYO645 2928135Z
PP NQ IP LS ME
DE NY 015
P 1800072 OCT 77
FM NEW YORK (196-66) (2 1)
TO DIRECTOR (87-14366) PRIORITY
INDIANAPOLIS (87-22 720) PRIORITY
LOUISVILLE (196-5) PRIORITY
MEMPHIS (87-16994) PRIORITY
BT
C L E A R
Frederick N. P. Pro, AKA - fugitive; et al; Elvis A. Presley (deceased) - victim; ITSP; FBW; WF; conspiracy, (OO: Memphis).
Re Memphis teletype to Bureau, October 13, 1977.

FREDERICK N. P. PRO, DOB - August 3, 1926, arrested by bureau agents on October 18, 1977, at 128 Central Park South New York (NY), NY, without incident. PRO was charged with violations of Title 16, Sections 1341, 2314, 1343 and 2, and 071.

PRO, upon advice of counsel, declined to discuss substantive charges.

NYO171 29422627
PP HQ IP MEE
DE NY 113
P 212128Z OCT 77

FM NEW YORK (196-66) (21)
TO DIRECTOR (87-143601) PRIORITY
INDIANAPOLIS (87-22726) PRIORITY
MEMPHIS (87-16994) PRIORITY
BT
C L E A R
FREDERICK N. P. PRO - Fugitive; et al; Elvis A.
Presley - (deceased) - victim; II SP; FBW; MF;
CONSPIRACY, OO:MEMPHIS
Re teletype to the bureau, dated October 16,
1977.
A USA Jacob Laufer, SD NY, advised that FRED-
ERICK PRO appeared before USM Kent Sinclair,
SO NY, at which time he posted at $15,000 check
as guarantee for $100,000 bail. USA Laufer stat-
ed this arrangement was agreeable to the USDCJ
in Memphis.
PRO waived removal hearing and will appear
USDC, Memphis, October 31, 1977.

Pro is given 48 hours to raise $100,000 in bail:

BSO883 2992145
RR NO ME
DE BS
R 262125Z OCT 77
PM BOSTON (196-13) (P)
TO DIRECTOR (87-143681) ROUTINE
MEMPHIS (87-16974) ROUTINE
BT
CLEAR
FREDERICK N. PRO; J. LAWRENCE WOLFSON;
RAYMOND W. BAZNER; GABRIEL ROBERT
CAGGIANO; ROY EVERETT SMITH; PHILIP KARL
KITZER; ELVIS A. PRSLEY (DECEASED) - VIC-
TIM; ITSP; FBW; MF; CONSPIRACY; OO: MEMPHIS
RE BOSTON TELETYPE, OCTOBER 15, 1977.
GABRIEL ROBERT CAGGIANO APPEARED
BEFORE U.S. MAGISTRATE RUDOLPH PIERCE ON
OCTOBER 25, 1977 AND WAIVED REMOVAL TO
MEMPHIS, TENNESSEE. MAGISTRATE PIERCE
ORDERED CAGGIANO TO SURRENDER HIMSELF
TO THE USA'S OFFICE IN MEMPHIS, TENNESSEE
NOT LATER THAN NOVEMBER 7, 1977.

PRO WAS ARRAIGNED BEFORE U.S. MAGIS-
TRATE KENT SINCLAIR, SDNY, THIS DATE, AND
WAS RELEASED ON HIS OWN RECOGNIZANCE
AND AFFORDED 48 HOURS TO RAISE $100,000
BAIL.

MM065B 2880031Z
RR HQ ME

DE MM
R 400310CT 77
FM MIAMI (196-68) P
TO DIRECTOR (87-143601) ROUTINE
MEMPHIS (87-16004) ROUTINE
BT
CLEAR
FREDERICK N. P. PRO - FUGITIVE (A); LAURENCE WOLFSON - FUGITIVE (A); RAYMOND W. BASZNER - FUGITIVE (A); GABRIEL ROBERT CAGGIANO - FUGITIVE (A); ROY EVERETT SMITH - FUGITIVE (A): PHILLIP KARL KITZER, JR. - FUGITIVE (A); ELVIS A. PRESLEY (DECEASED) - VICTIM; ITSP; FBW; MAIL FRAUD; CONSPIRACY; OO: MEMPHIS.

Re Memphis Teletype to director, October 13, 1977, and Memphis Telecal of SA to Miami, October 14, 1977.

Subjects, captioned above, known to be residing in Miami Division, and to be arrested by Miami upon direction of Bureau on October 17, 1977 as follows:

1. Laurence Wolfson, DOB October 13, 1916, age 61, address 2335 Biscayne Bay Drive, North Miami, Florida,

2. Raymond W. Blaszner, address 16390 Stonehaven Road, Miami Lakes, Florida,

3. Roy Everett Smith, DOB April 10, 1926, age 52, address 7947 Southwest 104th Street, Apartment C103, Miami, Florida.

UNITED STATES DEPARTMENT OF JUSTICE
FEDERAL BUREAU OFINVESTIGATION

Copy to: 1 - USA, SDNY (ATT: AUSA JACOB LAUFER)
1 - USA, Memphis

Report of: Office: New York, New York
Date:

Field Office File #: 1966-66   Bureau File #: 87-143601

Title: RAYMOND W. BAZNER;
GABRIEL ROBERT CAGGIANO;
PHILLIP KARL KITZER, JR.;
FREDERICK PETER PRO;
ROY EVERETT SMITH;
Character: J. LAWRENCE WOLFSON;
ELVIS A. PRESLEY (DECEASED) - VICTIM

Synopsis: INTERSTATE TRANSPORTATION OF STOLEN PROPERTY - FRAUD
BY WIRE - MAIL FRAUD - CONSPIRACY

FREDERICK PETER PRO, DOB 8/3/26, Philadelphia, Pa., (true name ALFREDO PROC), arrested on 10/18/77 at his place of business, 128 Central Park So., Apt. 4B, NYC, based on indictment returned Memphis, Tennessee, charging him with violation of Section 1341, 1343, 2314, 371, and 2, Title 18, USC. PRO, upon advice of counsel, declined to discuss charges. PRO arraigned 10/18/77 before USM KENT SINCLAIR, SDNY, released on his own recognizance, and afforded 48 hours to raise $100,000 bail. On 10/20/77, PRO again appeared before USM SIN-

CLAIR, at which time bail was fixed at $100,000, and PRO placed as guarantee a check in the amount of $15,000. PRO waived removal and agreed to appear before USDC, Memphis, on 10/31/77.

FREDERICK PETER PRO was placed under arrest by 8A at his place of business, Trident Consortium, 128 Central Park South, Apartment 4B, New York City (NYC), New York (NY). PRO was advised by 8A that his arrest was based upon a warrant issued by the United States District Court (USDC) Judge in Memphis, Tennessee. PRO immediately requested that he be allowed to consult his attorney and he was permitted to call his attorney from his place of business. Following the discussion with his attorney, PRO stated that upon advice of his attorney, he would decline to make any statement or comments other than to supply information concerning his identity and background.

PRO was verbally advised of his rights by 8A and while enroute to the New York Office (NYO) of the Federal Bureau of Investigation (FBI) shortly thereafter, he was furnished a form by 8A setting forth his rights. PRO read this form and indicated that he understood his rights, but he declined to sign the form.

PRO stated that his true complete name is FREDERICK PETER PRO, but through some way, unknown to him, his birth certificate erroneously carries his name as ALFREDO PROC. He said his mother and father, and his brothers and sisters have always been known as PRO.

Following is a description of PRO taken during

this interview:

       Name FREDERICK PETER PRO
       Sex   Male
       Race White
       Date of Birth   August 3, 1926
       Place of Birth   P h i l a d e l p h i a ,
Pennsylvania
       Height   6 foot
       Weight 180 pounds
       Eyes Brown
       Hair Gray
     Residence   128 Central Park South,
       Apartment 4B, New York
       City, telephone number
       (212) 582-1673, December, 00
       1976 to present
     Previous Addresses 4120 Kiaora Street
       Miami, Florida

       150 South Ocean Boulevard
       Palm Beach, Florida

       333 East 49th Street
       New York City, NY
     Employment Financial Consultant,
       presently President of
       Trident Consortium Funding
       Corporation, 128 Central
       Park South, Apartment
       4C, telephone number
       212-757-8037

    PRO advised that he was previously Vice-President and Program Manager of Budd

Company in NY and Philadelphia and did extensive work on the Metroliner and the Long island Railroad. He advised that he has also been president of the following companies:

Air Cargo Express
Miami, Florida;
Incorporated in Florida in January, 1976

Span East Airlines
Miami, Florida;
Incorporated in New York City

Parker West Corporation
Miami, Florida
Incorporated in Florida in July, 1974

Arrest Record Admits to no arrests

On October 18, 1977, FREDERIC, PETER PRO was arraigned before United States Magistrate (USM) KENT SINCLAIR, Southern District of new York (SDNY), at which time he was released upon his own recognizance and was given 48hours to raise the $100,000 bail recommended by United States District Judge ROBERT M. MC RAE, Memphis, Tennessee. PRO was requested, as a condition of this release, to maintain daily contact with pre-trial services, SDNY.

On October 21, 1977, Assistant United States Attorney (AUSA) JACOB LAUFER advised that FREDERICK PRO appeared before USM KENT SINCLAIR, SDNY, on October 20, 1977, at which time bail was fixed at $100,000, and PRO was permitted to place as a guarantee a check in the amount of $15,000. AUSA LAUFER advised that this was previously arranged with the United States District Court Judge in Memphis.

PRO at this time waived removal and agreed to appear before the United States District Court in Memphis on October 31, 1977.

Frederick N. P. Pro; J. Laurence Wolfson; Raymond W. Baszner; Gabriel Robert Caggiano; Roy Everett Smith; Philip Karl Kitzer, Jr.; Elvis A. Presley (deceased) - victim; ITSP; FBV; NF; conspiracy. OO: ME

RE Memphis teletype to the director, October 13, 1977.

On October 31, 1977, subject PRO appeared before WSDJ Harry W. Wellford, VDT, Memphis, Tenn., for arraignment and pleased not guilty to all charges contained in the Memphis indictment. He was represented by attorney Laurence Jeffrey Weingarde, 401 Broadway, New York City.

In seeking bond reduction from $100,000 secured, attorney Weingarde, in behalf of PRO, told the court that PRO was his proper name and that the name PROC on his birth certificate was a typographical error as both of his parents are named PRO. PRO is presently operating two businesses, Trident Consortium at New York City, which Weingarde stated is under investigation by the FBI, and also operates a business at Orlando, Fla., known as International Photographers Association. The abbreviation of this company is

IPC OPI IPC). IPC deals with photographing of recruits at the military bases in the surrounding areas. PRO is a veteran of the armed forces, having served in 1946-1947 and receiving an honorable discharge. He also studied for the priesthood at St. Charles Seminary, Landsdowne, Pa.

The USDJ ordered PRO's bond reduced from $100,000 to $75,000 secured. He required that in addition to the $15,000 already posted PRO post another $10,000 prior to leaving Memphis and in 6 weeks is to post an additional $25,000 cash or its equivalent and at the end of the second 6 weeks the necessity of the remaining one-third cash would be considered. PRO's passport is to be retained by the FBI which, according to the attorney, was seized at New York. We will be allowed to travel in the southern and eastern districts of New York, the western district of Tennessee, and within a 50 mile radius of Orlando, Fla. However, 5 days' notice in writing regarding travel to the state of Florida must be submitted. PRO is to report by noon on Tuesday and Friday weekly to the pre-trial services section, New York, and his travel must not interfere with these twice a week reports.

The Judge Fortner ruled that the $10,465 seized by FBI agents at New York may be applied toward the $25,000 initial secured deposit of his bond providing PRO can show legal possession of that money. Attorney Weingarde states that this money was sent to PRO by his company in Orlando, IPC and that they would submit affidavits from the company allowing him to use this money in connection with his bond.

PRO left Memphis with his attorney after signing appropriate papers of bail reform act and by Friday will be allowed to post the additional money required of the court to complete the first $25,000 installment on his bond.

It should be noted that PRO had an apparent limp which his attorney described as "pre-Phlebitis" and also had a bruise appearing below his left eye.

Investigation Memphis continuing.

This document summarizes the case—the language at the beginning of the document is such typical legal language that the theme music from the Jack Webb TV show "Dragnet" may echo in the background . . .

On October 13, 1977, the facts of this case were presented to the Federal Grand Jury, Western District of Tennessee, Memphis, Tennessee. Following deliberation, a sealed indictment was returned, which indictment remained sealed until October 18, 1977 when it was opened upon application of the United States Attorney's Office, Memphis. The indictment charged that FREDERIC, P. PRO, J. LAURENCE WOLFSON, RAYMOND BASZNER, GABRIEL ROBERT CAGGIANO, ROY EVERETT SMITH and PHILIP KARL KITZER, JR. devised and intended to devise a scheme and artifice to defraud and obtain money and property from ELVIS A. PRESLEY knowing that all representations made were false. The indictment sets forth that PRO did do business as Air Cargo Express, Inc. and as Span East Airlines, J. LAURENCE WOLFSON did business at Transworld Industries, RAYMOND W. BASZNER and GABRIEL ROBERT CAGGIANO did operate and control the business known as World Aircraft Exchange, Inc. and CAGGIANO acted as attorney for BASZNER and for World Aircraft Exchange. It was further part of the scheme to defraud ROY EVERETT SMITH, who acted as Secretary of the Board of Directors of and as Secretary of Air Cargo Express, Inc. and acted as an Agent of FREDERICK P. PRO.

In furtherance of this scheme, neither BASZN-ER nor CAGGIANO revealed to PRESLEY that they were employees of PRO nor did CAGGIANO reveal that he was a part owner of World Aircraft Exchange, Inc.

WOLFSON acted as Treasurer of Commercial Air Transport Sales, Inc. but did not reveal he did business as Transworld Industries, Inc.

By means of false pretenses and promises, PRESLEY sold his Lockheed Jetstar aircraft to WWP Aircraft Leasing Corporation, which in turn leased back the aircraft to PRESLEY for a monthly rental of $16,775 for 84 months. PRESLEY sub-leased the aircraft to Air Cargo Express for 84 months at a monthly rent of $17,775 and for an additional 36 months at a monthly rental of $10,000. At the same time WWP Leasing Corporation obtained a loan of $950,000 from the Chemical Bank of New York to finance the above transaction with $611,951.67 going to release PRESLEY's indebtedness to the American National Bank of Morristown, New Jersey. This indebtedness was only for aforementioned plane and the surplus of the loan, $338,048.33, would be used to finance the upgrading of this aircraft.

The indictment further notes that on June 25, 1976 and July 14, 1976 written lease agreements were executed. BASZNER agreed to report on the upgrading of the aircraft and PRO issued checks to PRESLEY in the amounts of $401,000, $17,755 and $17,755, all of which were subsequently determined to be worthless. Also, on June 25, 1976, PRO, WOLFSON and CAGGIANO left Memphis in PRESLEY's aircraft for Miami,

Florida.

In continuance of this scheme to defraud, PRO obtained money from PRESLEY never having performed any of the necessary modifications and PRO, as operator of Air Cargo Express, never made payments to PRESLEY required under the sub-lease terms of the contract. Also, PRO, WOLF-SON, BASZNER and CAGGIANO caused false and misleading invoices to be prepared in order to obtain money from PRESLEY, causing checks to be issued in amounts of \$129,500, \$17,500, \$117,500 and \$33,000. Also PRO and PHILIP KARL KITZER, JR. caused a false Telex message to be sent from Seven Oak Finance Limited, London, England, to the National Bank of Commerce, Memphis, Tennessee, reflecting that at the request of PRO the Seven Oak Finance had confirmed that Air Cargo Express had an account in excess of 500,000 U. S. dollars, knowing this statement to have been false. The subjects, on the 20th of July, 1976, caused a letter to be addressed to CHARLES H. DAVIS, attorney for PRESLEY, which was in violation of the Fraud by Mail Statute, Title 18, U. S. Code, Section 1341 and 2.

Count two notes that ROY SMITH caused a letter to be sent to CHARLES H. DAVIS in violation of the Fraud by Mail Statute.

In Count three, PRO is charged with violation of the Interstate Transportation of Stolen Property statute, Title 18, Section 2314, U. S. Code, with regard to taking the Lockheed Jetstar to Miami, Florida; count four identifies PRO as causing a Cashier's check, number 647716, in the amount of $32,000, drawn on the National Bank of Commerce, Memphis, Tennessee, and dated July 16, 1976, payable to Air Cargo Express, and a second Cashier's check, number 647717, payable to FREDERICK PRO, in the amount of $38,490, drawn on the National Bank of Commerce, Memphis, to be transported to Coral Gables, Florida; count five notes that PRO also caused the checks to be returned from Florida to Memphis, Tennessee, all in violation of the Interstate Transportation of Stolen Property Statute.

Similarly charged in count six is J. LAURENCE WOLFSON relative to the transportation to Ft. Lauderdale, Florida, Cashier's check number 647718, in the amount of $129,500, drawn on the National Bank of Commerce, Memphis, Tennessee, and dated July 16, 1976, which was payable to Transworld Industries, Inc. Count seven refers to the return of this check to Memphis, Tennessee and count six and seven are in violation of Title 18, Section 2314 and 2, U. S. Code.

Count eight of the indictment notes that BASZNER and CAGGIANO caused a Cashier's check, number 647719, drawn on the National Bank of Commerce, in the amount of $45,000, and dated July 16, 1976, payable to World Aircraft Exchange, Inc. to be transported to Boston, Massachusetts; and in count nine, they caused the transportation from Boston, Massachusetts to Memphis, Tennessee, both in violation of Title 18, Section 2314 and 2, U. S. Code.

Count ten identifies all the subjects causing transmission of telephone conversation between ROY SMITH and D. BEECHER SMITH, III between Miami, Florida and Memphis, Tennessee on or about August 27, 1976, and count eleven refers to a telephone communication between PRO and D. BEECHER SMITH which occurred between Miami, Florida and Memphis, Tennessee on August 27, 1976, both of which were in violation of the Fraud by Wire statute, Title 18, Section 1343 and 2, U. S. Code.

Count twelve referred to all subjects with regard to another telephone communication between Miami, Florida and Memphis, Tennessee on September 14, 1976 and also other communications in the month of September, 1976 between Memphis, Tennessee and Miami, Florida as well as on October 1, 1976 and October 4, 1976, all in violation of Title 18, Section 1343 and 2, U. S. Code, involving Fraud by Wire.

Count sixteen refers to a Telex message transmitted between Seven Oak Finance Limited, England, and the National Bank of Commerce, containing fraudulent contents, and this is in violation of the Fraud by Wire Statute also.

Count seventeen refers to the conspiracy between all the subjects in violation of Title 18, Sections 1341, 2314 and 2, and 371.

The indictment and warrants for arrest were all sealed under the Order of the U. S. District Judge ROBERT M. McRAE, Western District of Tennessee, Memphis, Tennessee, to be opened upon application by the United States Attorney to the District Court, whereupon the Clerk would be ordered to unseal the indictment.

By telephone communication on October 18, 1977, the Miami Division of the Federal Bureau of Investigation advised the Memphis Division that at approximately 5:00 p.m., Eastern Daylight Savings Time, PHILIP KARL KITZER was arrested by Special Agents and . This arrest was effected at Miami International Airport as KITZER arrived aboard Braniff International Airlines flight from the Republic of Panama.

Upon receiving this information, the Assistant U. S. Attorney, JOE A. DYCUS, Western District of Tennessee, Memphis, Tennessee, filed appropriate papers with U. S. District Court Judge McRAE and the indictment relative to the subject was unsealed by the Clerk, U. S. District Court, Western District of Tennessee. Orders were immediately dispatched to appropriate field divisions to arrest the individuals named in the indictment. By appropriate communication, the Miami Division advised that LAURENCE WOLFSON, white male, date of birth October 13, 1916, and residing at 2335 Biscayne Bay Drive, North Miami, Florida, was arrested October 18, 1977 by Bureau Agents without incident.

Attempts to arrest ROY E. SMITH in Miami at 7947 Southwest, 104th Street, Apartment C-103, were unsuccessful.

Additionally, it was determined that RAY-MOND W. BASZNER was not at his residence or at Classical Automotive, his employment.

On October 20, 1977, RAYMOND W. BASZNER surrendered to FBI Agents of the Miami Division and appeared before U. S. Magistrate PETER R.

PALERMO. He was released on $10,000 personal surety bond. He was represented by Attorney VINCENT FLYNN and waived formal removal hearing.

PHILIP KARL KITZER appeared before U. S. Magistrate PALERMO, Miami, Florida, on October 31, 1977, at which time bond was set at $100,000 corporate surety and $50,000 corporate surety respectively for cases emanating from Louisville, Kentucky and Memphis, Tennessee. KITZER was remanded to the custody of the U.S. Marshal, Miami, to await removal proceedings.

Subsequently, on October 20, 1977, KITZER was afforded an identity hearing before U. S. Magistrate SORRENTINO, Miami, Florida, at which time he waived removal proceedings for the indictment pending out of Memphis, Tennessee. Attorney JAY MOSKOWITZ, Miami Strike Force, advised Magistrate SORRENTINO that an arrangement was scheduled for KITZER to be in Louisville, Kentucky on November 3, 1977 and subsequent to the identity hearing, KITZER was remanded to the custody of the U.S. Marshal, Miami, Florida, to be incarcerated at the federal Correctional Institute, Dade County, Florida.

By appropriate communication, the Boston Division advised that GABRIEL ROBERT CAGGIANO was arrested on October 18, 1977 at Boston, Massachusetts by Special Agents of the Federal Bureau of Investigation. A bond hearing was held before U. S. Magistrate RUDOLPH PIERCE and bond was set at $2,500 surety.

By appropriate communication, the New York Division advised that FREDERICK W. P. PRO, a white male, date of birth August 3, 1926, was arrested by Special Agents of the Federal Bureau of Investigation on October 18, 1977, at 128 Central Park South, New York City. PRO, upon advice of counsel, declined to discuss substantive charges. He was arraigned before U. S. Magistrate KENT SINCLAIR, Southern District of New York, and was released on his own recognizance and afforded 48 hours to raise $100,000 bail.

PRO subsequently appeared before U. S. District Judge HARRY WELLFORD, Western District of Tennessee, Memphis, Tennessee, and was represented by Attorney LAWRENCE JEF-FREY WEINGARD, 401 Broadway, New York City. PRO entered a not guilty plea to all counts.

Through his attorney, he advised the court, in an effort for bond reduction, that he had worked for Budd Company of Philadelphia in the construction of railroad cars for ten years and was Vice-President of the program for the implementation of the Metro Liner Service.

The name PROC on his birth certificate is a typographical error as both his parents are named PRO, and he constantly uses the name PRO.

PRO presently has two businesses he runs, one the Trident Consortium, New York City, which, according to the attorney, is presently under investigation by the New York Office of the Federal Bureau of Investigation. In addition, he has a company known as IPC representing International Photographers Company which is based in Orlando, Florida and deals with the photographing of recruits at the various military bases.

PRO is allegedly a veteran with the Armed Forces during the period of 1946 - 1947, receiving an honorable discharge. He also entered St. Charles Seminary, at Landsdown, Pennsylvania, to study for the priesthood.

PRO complained, through his attorney, of having a pre-flebitis which caused his problems in his legs and requires treatment. In addition, the FBI seized $10,460 from him which was money forwarded to PRO by his company, IPC, which is in Orlando and was forwarded to PRO at New York.

After hearing various information furnished by PRO, United States District Judge ruled that the $100,000 bond on PRO should be reduced to $75,000 and that the $15,000 check already provided by PRO should be supplemented by another $10,000 prior to his departure from Memphis. He can, if so desired, according to the court, apply the monies seized in connection with the search warrant in New York, to the $25,000 if it is legitimate money of PRO and not someone else's money.

After six weeks, he will be required to post the second third of the $75,000 bond, that is another $25,000. His passport, which was taken from him at New York shall be retained in the custody of the U. S. He is to give five days notice in writing regarding travel which he may take to the state of Florida and in Florida he must stay within a 50 mile radius of Orlando, the site of his business. He is allowed to retain his travel status in the Southern and Eastern districts of New York and come to the Western District of Tennessee when required by the court.

On October 20, 1977, ROY EVERETT SMITH, white male, date of birth April 10, 1925, surrendered at the U. S. Marshal's office, Miami, Florida. He posted a $10,000 surety bond, and on October 21, 1977 appeared before U. S. Magistrate PETER R. PALERMO, U. S. District Court, Southern District of Florida, Miami, Florida, for his initial appearance. He waived at removal proceedings and SMITH was given permission to travel within the continental United States based upon needs of his work.

On October 25, 1977, GABRIEL ROBERT CAGGIANO appeared before U. S. Magistrate RUDOLPH PIERCE, Boston, Massachusetts, and waived removal to Memphis, Tennessee. CAGGIANO was to surrender himself to the United States Attorney's Office, Memphis, no later than November 7, 1977.

The following investigation was conducted by SA of the Memphis Division:

On November 1, 1977, Memphis, Tennessee, telephone was contacted regarding the location of a travel firm known as Welch Travel. a member of the American Society of Travel Agents, reviewed his copy of that association's directory and determined that the following listings could be identical with Welch Travel:

VALEDA M. WELCH, Welch Travel, 1012 Ralston Avenue, Defiance, Ohio, telephone (419) 782-3821;

DEBORAH WELCH, Shirley House of Travel, 21 North Scokie boulevard, Lake Bluff, Illinois, telephone (312) 234-0720.

On November 1, 1977, a confidential source of the Memphis Division advised that his records reflect two listings under the heading Welch Travel as follows:

Welch Travel, 1012 Ralston Avenue, Defiance, Ohio;

Welch Travel consultants, Inc., 15 Walnut Street, Wellesley, Massachusetts.

On 9/20/77, a series of search warrants were executed at key locations throughout the United States at the residences and businesses of primary subjects related to OPFOPEN. The two additional cases captioned in the title of this communication are considered OPFOPEN related. One of these searches was conducted at Bannon International, 156 State Street, Boston, Massachusetts. The Boston Division seized a voluminous amount of records stored at this establishment and thereafter began to put the information in a form suitable for entry into the computer system (Major Case Information System).

At the present time, Boston is continuing to review the seized material and is in the process of setting forth leads based on information obtained form the material.

As brief background:

Beginning on 12/16/74, and extending through 1975, PHILLIP KARL KITZER, JR. and other individuals operated an "off shore bank" identified as the First National City Bank and Trust Company, Ltd., Granada, West Indies. From approximately 11/75 through 5/76, KITZER was a leading figure in the operation of a second "off shore" bank, the Mercantile Bank and Trust Company, St. Vincent, and Chicago, Illinois. With increasing law enforcement interest in each of the aforenamed "off shore" banks, KITZER and his associates moved to create anew vehicle for fraud. The third "off shore" bank organized was the Seven Oak Finance, Ltd. Bank in Kent, England, which KITZER and his associates had acquired by the Fall of 1976. It is reasonably estimated through comments made by KITZER that the total amount of fraudulent negotiable instruments written through the "off shore" banks operated by KITZER and his associates, approximates 21/2 billion dollars. In all three of these ventures, KITZER and others sold and/or were involved in the negotiation of letters of credit, certificates of deposit, loan guarantees and other financial instruments on these "off shore" banks.

KITZER and his associates have termed themselves, "The Fraternity" and are a loosely knit group comprised of approximately 30 to 40 of the world's top con-men. These con-men have maintained contact with each other through the extensive use of telephones, telex machines, the mail and personal visits.

Frederick Pro's fingerprints are examined by the FBI's Laboratory, in Washington, D.C.:

FBI

LABORATORY

FEDERAL BUREAU OF INVESTIGATION

WASHINGTON, D. C. 20535

To: SAC, Miami (196-68)   February   24, 1977

From: Director, FBI FBI FILE NO. 87-143601
      FREDERICK N. P. PRO; LAB NO. 80201002 D
SP
      ET AL;
Re: ELVIS A. PRESLEY (DECEASED) - VICTIM;
      ITSP; MF;
      FBW; CONSPIRACY
      OO: Memphis

Examination requested by: Miami

Reference: Airtel dated January 24, 1978

Examination requested: Document- Fingerprint

Remarks:

If additional examinations are desired in this matter concerning Q1 through Q9, it is suggested that handwriting exemplars be acquired from any logical suspect. These exemplars should consist of examples of all questioned writing appearing on the questioned specimens and should be sufficiently numerous to represent the writing ability of the writer. The exemplars should be prepared on paper corresponding in size and general format to the questioned specimens.

REPORT
Of the
FBI
LABORATORY
FEDERAL BUREAU OF INVESTIGATION
WASHINGTON, D. C. 20535

To: SAC, Miami (196-68) February 24, 1978

      FBI FILE NO. 87-143601

      FREDERICK N. P. PRO;   LA NO. 80201002
D SP
      ET AL;
Re: ELVIS A. PRESLEY (DECEASED) - VICTIM;
      ITSP; MF;
      FBW; CONSPIRACY

Specimens received   January 31, 1978

Nine sheets of paper bearing handwritten notations, further described as follows:
Q1   Sheet with notations beginning "Do you have . . ."
Q2   Sheet with notations beginning "Guess What has . . ."
Q3   Sheet with notations beginning "Miami

now has . . ."

Q4   Sheet with notations beginning "gally
Bar . . ."

Q5   Sheet with notations beginning "Supreme
Jet Service . . ."

Q6   Sheet with notations beginning "Should
you have . . ."

Q7   Sheet with notations beginning "NonStop -
New York . . ."

Q8   Sheet with notations beginning "Hello,
we would like . . ."

Q9   Sheet with notations beginning " 99
passengers . . ."

Result of examination:

Due to the limited nature of comparable letters and letter combinations in the questioned writing and handwriting variations observed in the comparison of portions of the questioned writing, it could not be determined whether the questioned writing on Q1 through Q9 was or was not prepared by the same writer or writers.

The available known writing of FREDERICK P. PRO, FBI consisting of signatures on fingerprint cards, is not sufficiently comparable with the questioned writing on Q1 through Q9 for adequate examination.

The submitted evidence has been photographed and will be returned with the result of the latent fingerprint examination.

In over 660 pages of FBI files related to Elvis Presley, the final disposition of the Jetstar larceny case by Frederick Pro may have been stated. If it was, that material has been blacked out. The files do not now reveal the final outcome of the case against Frederick Pro. Nor do the files indicate the final whereabouts the Jetstar aircraft.

The final case in the FBI files concerns a red 1955 Chevrolet Corvette, VIN VE55S001102, purchased by Elvis Presley from the (now-defunct) Don Allen Chevrolet dealership in New York City for the 1955 price of $3,864. According to the dealership invoice, the Corvette as equipped with: 195 H.P. "Turbo Fire V8," "3 speed manual transmission," "Wonderbar Radio (Signal Seeking)," trunk mats and floor mat.

The Corvette was much later sold via a national auto auction firm for at least $34,000. Any vehicle owned by Elvis Presley quickly appreciated in value to a huge extent — and existing Presley automobiles command very high prices at auction or sale.

The purchaser, of Oelwein, Iowa later complained to officials that the sale may have constituted interstate fraud because he claimed that 1955 model Corvettes didn't have the radio and transmission specified.

That complaint triggered an extensive FBI investigation, including dealer records at the Don Allen dealership, a complete 1955 Corvette parts catalog, correspondence with the New Jersey Motor Vehicles department, correspondence with Iowa and Omaha FBI offices, the Iowa Attorney

General's Office and the U.S. Department of Justice. One Presley cousin and employee in Memphis was quoted (third from bottom paragraph, last document, following) as saying she didn't remember Presley ever owning a Corvette.

There are at least 70 pages of documents in the Presley file regarding the 1965 Corvette. The pages following are typical of the FBI investigations into this possible fraud case:

Date: 4/2/81

Subject: 1955 CHEVROLET CORVETTE CONVERTIBLE, VIN VE55S001102, FORMERLY OWNED BY ELVIS PRESLEY, VALUED AT $34,000 ITSP (B)
        00: Omaha

To: DIRECTOR, FBI
    (ATTN: FBI LABORATORY)

For the information of the FBI Laboratory, the Omaha Division is currently investigating captioned ITSP matter to determine if a fraud has occurred regarding the sale of a 1955 Chevrolet Corvette convertible automobile purportedly owned by Elvis Presley in Atlantic City, New Jersey, in February of 1979. The present owner of this automobile, of Oelwein, Iowa, paid $34,000 for the Corvette at the auction in Atlantic City, New Jersey. Previous owners furnished the auction with an original bill of sale and an original invoice for the vehicle, which were both dated in January of 1955, and the Corvette was sold by the Don Allen Chevrolet dealership of New York City to Presley. Individuals at the 2/19/79 Atlantic City, New Jersey, car auction purported that the bill of sale for the vehicle, which was signed by Presley, was found under the seat of the automobile by individuals restoring the car some years ago.

After the owner returned to Oelwein, Iowa, with the Corvette, an article appeared in the "Old Cars Weekly newspaper approximately six months later indicating that the Elvis Presley Corvette was a fraud because of the fact that the car had a three-speed manual transmission and a Wonder Bar radio. These options were not available to the Corvette in January of 1955 when Presley supposedly purchased it. The current owner wants to determine if he is the victim of a fraud in this matter, or if the Corvette is, in fact, a vehicle that was owned by Elvis Presley. If the Corvette was, in fact, Presley's car, its value would be many times greater than if it was not Presley's car.

The U. S. Attorney's Office at Cedar Rapids, Iowa, believes that a violation of Title 18, Section 2314, may have been committed in that the current owner was required to travel interstate to purchase the car and that the sellers knew that the vehicle was a fraud.

REQUEST OF THE FBI LABORATORY
DOCUMENT EXAMINATION SECTION
It is requested that the FBI Laboratory, Document Examination Section, inform Omaha if it is possible to examine the type on the original invoice or

bill of sale for the Corvette convertible to tell whether or not the typewriter was manufactured prior to or subsequent to 1955.

It is also requested that the FBI Laboratory advise Omaha of the feasibility of determining the age of the paper on which the bill of sale and invoice were printed. The current owner of the automobile would relinquish these documents to have them examined by the FBI Laboratory if it were felt that such examination might be able to prove the age of the documents.

Date: 6/10/81

     SAC, PHILADELPHIA (87B-28890) (NSRA) (RUC)

Subject: 1955 CHEVROLET CORVETTE
         CONVERTIBLE,
To: VIN VE55S00102, FORMERLY OWNED BY
     ELVIS PRESLEY, VALUED AT $34,000,
     ITSP (B)
     OO:OM)

     SAC, OMAHA (87-18813)

Re Omaha letter to New York and Philadelphia, 4/13/81.

Enclosed for Omaha is a copy of a bill of sale #15208, concerning a 1955 Corvette purchased by Elvis Presley on 1/18/55 from Don Allen Chevrolet, 1775 Broadway, New York, NY. Also enclosed for Omaha is the original and one copy each of an investigative insert reflecting investigation conducted at Newtown Square, PA, and an FD-302 reflecting interview with on 5/20/81 at West Chester, PA.

West Chester, PA, West Chester, PA, telephone was contacted at the office of and furnished the following information:

On February 18, 1978, attended the Kruse Auction in Atlantic City, NJ, during which time registered a 1955 Chevrolet Corvette with Kruse and representing the car by publicly announcing that it had originally belonged to Elvis Presley and that he was selling same. Further announced that he had the original bill of sale with Presley's name on it that was mounted on a plaque which he displayed. The bill of sale looked authentic to and he had no reason to believe that the car was not one of Elvis Presley's former automobiles and that he bought the car based on the Elvis Presley bill of sale.

Subsequently bidded $17,500 for the Corvette which bid was accepted. He paid Kruse for the car by check which cleared and received the bill of sale at the time of purchase. stated that he received no other paper work other than the Presley bill of sale. had never met prior to the purchase of the car and has had no contact with him since. kept the Corvette for a year during which he kept it in a garage except for displaying it at a custom car show in Philadelphia, PA, for which he received no money. He trailered the car to and from the show in a covered trailer. When purchased the car it had a three-speed transmission. He does not remember anything concerning the car's radio. He stated that there was nothing irregular about the car and that he made no physical changes to the car whatsoever with the exception of improving it's cleanliness.

Furnished a copy of the above mentioned bill of sale to Special Agent which indicates that on January 18, 1955, Presley, 103 Audobon Drive, Memphis, TN, purchased a new 1955 red Chevrolet Corvette, VIN VE55S001102 from Don Allen Chevrolet, 1775 Broadway, New York, NY, for $3,864, bill of sales #15208, invoice #SS-203.

The following investigation was conducted by Special Agent at Newtown Square, PA.

On May 8, 1981, a review of the 1980 Bell Telephone Company of Pennsylvania, Alphabetical Telephone Directory for West Chester, PA, disclosed two listings for West Chester, PA, non published telephone number.

Mr. James H. Reynolds
United States Attorney
Cedar Rapids, Iowa

        Attention: Mr. Robert L. Teig
              Assistant United States Attorney
      Re: Purchase of a 1955 Chevrolet
Corvette
              Convertible with Vehicle Identification
              Number VE55S001102 by
              Of Oelwein, Iowa

Dear Mr. Reynolds:

The purpose of this letter is to confirm a telephone conversation between Special Agent (SA) of our Waterloo, Iowa, Office and Mr. Robert L. Teig of your Cedar Rapids, Iowa, Office on September 23, 1981, at which time the following facts were presented to Mr. Teig:

In February of 1981, the Consumer Protection Division of the Iowa Department of Justice, Des Moines, Iowa, requested the assistance of the FBI regarding a possible interstate fraud violation which occurred when Mr. of Oelwein, Iowa, purchased a red 1955 Chevrolet Corvette automobile at the Kruse Antique Car Auction in Atlantic City, New Jersey, in February of 1979. paid $34,000 for the automobile, which was sold as a car previously owned by Elvis Presley. According to documents furnished with the car at the time of the auction, the corvette was sold to Elvis Presley of Memphis, Tennessee, on January 18, 1955, for $3,864. The automobile had a 195-horsepower "Turbo Fire V8" engine with a three-speed manual transmission and a Wonderbar signal-seeking radio.

After returned to Oelwein, Iowa, with the car, he received several letters from Corvette enthusiasts throughout the United States informing him that the car was not equipped with original options as indicated on the bill of sale, because those options (the three-speed manual transmission and the Wonderbar radio) were not available in January of 1955.

1-USA, Cedar Rapids, IA
1-Mr. Gene Battani, Consumer Protection Division
Iowa State Department of Justice
1-Omaha (87B-18813)

In order to determine if there was a fraud committed by the previous owner of the automobile or by the auction in New Jersey concerning the claim that the automobile belonged to Elvis Presley, the following investigation was conducted:

Mr. of Basking Ridge, New Jersey, one of the automobile's former owners, advised that he purchased the Corvette approximately five years ago from a Newark, New Jersey, car dealer for $3,000 cash. indicated the car had been advertised in the New York Times newspaper. stated he did not renovate the car in any way, and he sold the car to for $2,000.

Aadvised that he only provided with the title to the car; and he did not claim that the car was ever owned by Elvis Presley, nor did he furnish any invoice or documents which would make this claim.

Of Neponsit, New York, was interviewed and he claims he paid $4,000 for the automobile from an unknown individual in New Jersey. stated that he put $10,000 of his own money into the car before he sold it. claims that he received a bill of sale from the man in New Jersey which indicated that the Corvette had been previously owned by Elvis Presley. advised that he mounted and laminated the invoice, but he was not sure in his own mind that the car had, indeed, belonged to Presley.

Stated he did not change the vehicle's transmission, nor did he install a signal-seeking radio in the car. Both of these features were on the car prior to his purchase.

Advised that he sold the automobile to through the Kruse Auto Auction and provided the laminated document showing that the vehicle previously was owned by Elvis Presley to at the time of the sale.

Stated that he was not able to provide positively that the car had previously been owned by Elvis Presley and if he would have been able to do that, he would have sold the automobile for $100,000.

Of West Chester, Pennsylvania, advised that he purchased the Corvette on February 18, 1978, from through the Kruse Auto Auction and he paid $17,500 for the car. advised that in his opinion, claimed that the car was Elvis Presley's at the time he purchased it and he even provided a laminated bill of sale at that time.

Advised that he did not physically change the automobile in anyway, and he sold it one year later through the Kruse Auto Auction to of Oelwein, Iowa.

The FBI Laboratory in Washington D. C. examined the car invoice from Don Allen Chevrolet of New York New York, which indicated that the automobile was sold to Elvis Presley on January 18, 1955. Because the document was laminated by a previous owner, the document itself could not be subjected to several tests which could be performed on paper. The FBI Laboratory examiner located several apparent irregularities, in the invoice; however, without an original Don Allen Chevrolet Company invoice to compare the document to, the examiner was unable to say if the document was a fake or a forgery. (The Don Allen Chevrolet Company is no longer in business.)

An inquiry at the Chevrolet Corvette Manufacturing Plant in Saint Louis, Missouri, determined that the three-speed manual transmission and the Wonderbar signal-seeking radio were, indeed, options that could have been purchased in January of 1955.

A review was made of the vehicles titled to Elvis Presley of Memphis, Tennessee, by the Motor Vehicle Revenue Department for the State of Tennessee in Memphis; and as a result of this review, it was concluded that Presley never titled a Corvette automobile in the State of Tennessee. Most of the vehicles titled by Presley in the State of Tennessee were larger, luxury cars, trucks, and motorcycles.

Contact was made with the E. H. Crump Insurance Company of Memphis, Tennessee: This company has handled Insurance for Elvis Presley and his estate for over 15 years. The company did not have any record of Presley ever owning a Chevrolet Corvette automobile.

A cousin of Elvis Presley and an employee of the Presley estate, said that Presley, to her knowledge, never bought or owned any Corvette convertibles.

After hearing the above facts, Mr. Teig advised that it is very doubtful the FBI investigation could ever meet the requirements of Title 18, Section 2314, USC, regarding fraudulent claims or inducements by the former owners of the automobile, which caused to travel interstate to purchase the vehicle. Based on Mr. Teig's decision, no further investigation will be conducted in this matter by the FBI.

On November 24, 1981, a synopsis of the FBI's investigation was discussed with at the FBI Office in Waterloo, Iowa. All of the original evidence belonging to originally provided by the State of Iowa, Department of Justice, was turned over to at that time.

Very Truly Yours,

Herbert H. Hawkins, Jr.
Special Agent in Charge

By:
Supervisory Special Agent

FBI investigations at the Chevrolet manufacturing plant in St. Louis, Mo., where the Corvette was built indicated that the "Wonderbar" radio and the transmission in question could have, in fact, been installed in Corvettes during the time the 1955 Corvette was built, therefore no fraud case could be proved.

Thus the Elvis Presley FBI ends; a sordid trail of death threats, citizen complaints, the extortion attempt, the larceny by trick of his executive airplane, and the alleged fraud of the automobile.

All behind the scenes, largely hidden from the public. None of this was Presley's fault, but a huge file, nonetheless. And this does not include files kept by other agencies, state and local.

This record mirrors, we can be sure, other stars of Presley's stature. The threats, the larcenies, extortion attempts, frauds, theft.

All this can be summed up in a few words: the price of status; the cost of fame.

Appendix

The following pages are examples of documents in the Elvis Presley FBI files:

1, 2, 3, 4 5: alleged death threat, 1959, sent to RCA Victor records. Attempt on his life by (East?) German Red (Communist) soldier, when Presley was in the military service.

6, 7, 8: Letter from Laurens Johannes Griessel-Landau, 1959, to Presley before beginning "treatments" and before an extortion attempt.

9, 10, 11, 12: Postal card death threat, 1964, and reaction by the FBI because the postal card mentioned "JBJ," presumably LBJ, Lyndon Baines Johnson.

13, 14: Aug. 1970. Death threat in Las Vegas and mention in "BUFILES" (Bureau Files) of paternity suit.

15, 16, 17: Briefing papers about the tour given Presley, six colleagues and William Morris, former Sheriff, Shelby County, Tennessee, when they toured FBI headquarters. Note that Presley indicated that "he is of the opinion that the Beatles laid the groundwork for many of the problems we are having with young people by their filthy unkempt appearances and suggestive music while entertaining in his country during the early and middle 1960s. He advised that the Smothers Brothers, Jane Fonda and other persons in the entertainment industry of their ilk have a lot to answer for in the hereafter for the way they have poisoned young minds by disparaging the United States in their public statements and unsavory activities." (page 2) J. Edgar Hoover refused (politely) to meet with Presley, thus the FBI tour was given by others.

18: 1977—the fraud case of the Presley airplane. This page indicates how heavily redacted (edited; blacked out) some of these pages are.

19, 20: internal FBI report almost completely redacted before being released to the public.

21: The FBI issues documents clarifying that Frederick Pro may also be known as Frederick Proc.

22: page inserted when an original page is deleted from FBI files, before they are made public.

23, 24: Frederick Pro becomes a fugitive; bond is revoked.

25: Pro's colleagues are arrested without incident.

26: Frederick Pro charged with Mail Fraud, Interstate Transportation of Stolen Property, Money taken by Fraud, Wire Fraud and Conspiracy in the Presley aircraft case.

27-36: records in the alleged fraud case of the 1955 Corvette, purchased by Presley.

Canton
3 - // - 59

Dear Sir

I have just read a letter
from a relation in
West Germany.

Plans have been made &
already in the Hands of
a red soldier in East Germany
to kill Elvis Presley.
The mans own sister signed
a not in the West Germany
She read the Plans & is
not in favor of what her
brother is being Paid to
do. This red soldier will be

wearing an american
uniform — he is to leave
east Germany slip in to
west Germany some time
between mar 14 + 22nd
he has been given orders
to kill him even if he
has to blow up the
Hotel or home where he &
his father lives.
Please Please dont take
this as a crank letter
because as god is my
witness this every word
is true — I can not give

my name as the relatives
name in Germany the
People in aust germany
would be in danger
and of course the sister
would be killed.
I had thought of writing
to the President as some
Government officeal - but I
felt they would just
consider it a letter from
crank + forget it.
as you have a contract
with Presley + know his
manager so well. maybe

you can get some
action. I am not a
teenager I am a mother
& Grandmother

Please try to Protect
This young american soldier
in whatevery way you
can.

Thank you

NB Please note New address.

I Laurinz J. Landau.
c/o Mrs M. E. Landau.
"ELandsKoal Farm",
P. O. Mooinooi
Via - Pretoria.
Transvaal.
South Africa.
26/10/59.

To Mr Elvis Presley,

Dear Elvis, Trusting that
this note reaches you in good health
and in fine spirits. May I inform
you that I have cancelled many
New bookings. and that I have
completed all arrangements
for my departure to Germany.

FOR OFFICIAL USE ONLY

135

II

and I shall meet you upon
your return from Wildflecken
so that you will be able to
start with your treatments almost
immediately. Also, I feel honored
and very privileged in having
been chosen for this important
task. In fact, I am greatly
enthused in my mission and
assure you, as you are soon
to see, that I am going to
work wonders with your skin.
It is certainly my cherished
ambition to give you a complete
new skin and I swear to achieve
this within the quickest possible

3.

Time. I shall spare myself no efforts in this direction.

Please convey to your very good and charming secretary my sincerest thanks for all her kind attentions. As you would say with your sense of Humour "Miss Postage Stamp" must be overworked what with all the Mail. Bless Her. Enclosed find Latest clipping from our Weekend Local paper. Au Revoir & best wishes,

Yrs. Truly.

Lawton.

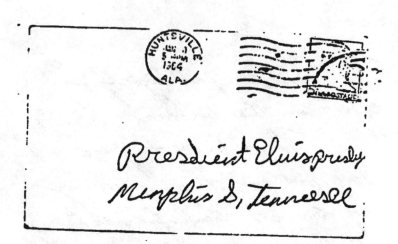

President Eluispresly
Menphis S, Tenneesel

Recorded
1/20/64
gta

FEDERAL BUREAU OF INVESTIGATION
UNITED STATES DEPARTMENT OF JUSTICE

Laboratory Work Sheet

No Lab File

Re: Unsub   aka ~~███████~~ b $7C$ File #   9-41793-
      ~~████~~   ELVIS PRESLEY PRESLEY -   Lab. #   D-440449 IK
      ·Victim
      EXTORTION: POSSIBLE THREAT TO
      PRESIDENT OF THE UNITED STATES

Examination requested by: Memphis (9-New)   1/15/64

Examination requested: Document   Date received: 1/17/64

Result of Examination: Examination by: ~~████~~

b $7C$

Specimens submitted for examination

Q1   Post card postmarked "HUNTSVILLE ALA. JAN 10 1964
     5 30 PM" bearing handwritten address "Presdient Elvis
     Presly Memphis S, Tennessee" bearing on reverse side
     handwritten note beginning "You Will Be next on my
     list..."

140

FD-36 (Rev. 12-13-56)

F B I

Date: 2/20/64

Transmit the following in _____
                                    (Type in plain text or code)

Via ___AIRTEL___

                                    (Priority or Method of Mailing)

TO: DIRECTOR, FBI

FROM: SAC, MEMPHIS (9-1231) (C)

UNSUB, AKA ███████████████████
ELVIS PRESLEY - VICTIM
EXTORTION; POSSIBLE THREAT TO PRESIDENT
OF UNITED STATES

        Re Bureau Airtel to Memphis, 2/19/64.

        There is enclosed original of post card postmarked
Huntsville, Ala., Jan. 10, 1964, 5:30 PM, bearing handwritten
address, "President Elvis Presly   Memphis 5, tennessee," and
bearing on the reverse side handwritten note, "You will be
nest on my list...."

        The enclosed post card was forwarded to the Bureau
with Memphis Airtel 1/15/64, captioned as above, and was
returned to Memphis by the FBI Laboratory by Laboratory Report
dated 1/20/64. The enclosure is for referral to U. S. Secret
Service, Washington, D. C.

③ - Bureau (Enc.-1) (RM)
1 - Memphis
COH:ME
(4)

                              REC-123 9-

                    FEB 1

Approved: _____ Sent _____ M Per _____
          Special Agent in Charge

FBI

FEDERAL BUREAU OF INVESTIGATION
COMMUNICATIONS SECTION
AUG 29 1970
TELETYPE

NR 223 LA PLAIN

3116 PM SITEL 8-28-70 WLB

TO DIRECTOR

LAS VEGAS

FROM LOS ANGELES (9-NEW)(P) 1P

Unknown Subject

UNSUB: ELVIS PRESLEY - VICTIM, EXTORTION.

RE LA TEL TODAY.

_____ RECEIVED TELCALL FROM SAME INDIVIDUAL WHO CALLED HER EARLY IN THE MORNING THIS DATE. CALL WAS RECEIVED AT TWELVE NOON AND CALLER STATED HE HAS THE CAR LICENSE NUMBER AND NAME OF INDIVIDUAL WHO IS GOING TO KILL ELVIS PRESLEY. THIS INDIVIDUAL HAS DEPARTED FROM LA AND HAS A RESERVATION FOR SAT. EVENING PERFORMANCE OF PRESLEY. CALLER REQUESTED "FIFTY THOUSAND GRAND BONUS" FOR INFO RE IDENTITY AND LICENSE NUMBER OF KILLER. IDENTIFIED THIS INDIVIDUAL AS PERSON WHO IS CRAZY AND ONE WHO COULD BE ON LSD. CALLER TERMINATED PHONE CALL ABRUPTLY STATING HE WOULD CALL BACK WITH FURTHER DETAILS. HE MADE NO INSTRUCTIONS RE PAYOFF. AS OF NINE PM, PDT, LA TIME, CALLER HAS NOT RECONTACTED _____

LAS VEGAS

LV INSURE ABOVE INFO IS FURNISHED TO LOCAL AUTHORITIES AND PERSONNEL ASSOCIATED WITH THE PRESLEY GROUP. LA IS MAINTAINING CONTACT WITH _____

PENDING.

END

M. A. Jones to Bishop Memo
RE: ELVIS PRESLEY

ever have need of his services he can be reached under the pseudonym of
Colonel Jon Burrows, 3764 Highway 51, South, Memphis, Tennessee,
telephone number XX X17.

INFORMATION IN BUFILES:

   Bufiles reflect that Presley has been the victim in a number
of extortion attempts which have been referred to the Bureau. Our files
also reflect that he is presently involved in a paternity suit pending in
Los Angeles, California, and that during the height of his popularity during
the latter part of the 1950's and early 1960's his gyrations while performing
were the subject of considerable criticism by the public and comment in
the press.

RECOMMENDATION:

   For information.

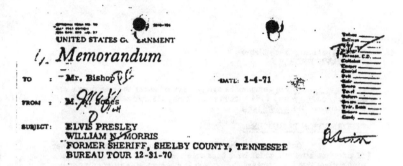

UNITED STATES GOVERNMENT

1. Memorandum

TO : Mr. Bishop

DATE: 1-4-71

FROM : M. A. Jones

SUBJECT: **ELVIS PRESLEY**
WILLIAM N. MORRIS
FORMER SHERIFF, SHELBY COUNTY, TENNESSEE
BUREAU TOUR 12-31-70

Presley and Morris and six individuals who provide security for Presley visited FBI Headquarters and were afforded a very special tour of our facilities in accordance with plans approved by the Director.

Regrets were expressed to Presley and his party in connection with their request to meet the Director. Presley indicated that he has long been an admirer of Mr. Hoover, and has read material prepared by the Director including "Masters of Deceit," "A Study of Communism" as well as "J. Edgar Hoover on Communism." Presley noted that in his opinion no one has ever done as much for his country as has Mr. Hoover, and that he, Presley, considers the Director the "greatest living American." He also spoke most favorably of the Bureau.

Despite his rather bizarre personal appearance, Presley seemed a sincere, serious minded individual who expressed concern over some of the problems confronting our country, particularly those involving young people. In this regard, in private comments made following his tour, he indicated that he, Presley, is the "living proof that America is the land of opportunity" since he rose from truck driver to prominent entertainer almost overnight. He said that he spends as much time as his schedule permits informally talking to young people and discussing what they consider to be their problems with them. Presley feels that long hair and unusual apparel were merely tools of his trade and provided him access to and rapport with many people particularly on college campuses who considered themselves "anti-establishment." Presley said that while he has a limited education, he has been able to command a certain amount of respect and attention from this segment of the population and in an informal way point out the errors of their ways. He advised that he does not consider himself

Enclosure 1-4-71   RLG 79
1 - Mr. Sullivan - Enclosure   1 - Miss Gandy - Enclosure
1 - Mr. Bishop - Enclosure   1 - Miss Holmes - Enclosure
1 - C. D. Brennan - Enclosure   1 - M. A. Jones - Enclosure
GTQ:dkg (9)   (CONTINUED - OVER)

5 JAN 13 1970

144

M. A. Jones to Bishop Memo
RE: ELVIS PRESLEY

competent to address large groups but much rather prefers small gatherings in community centers and the like, where he makes himself accessible for talks and discussions regarding the evils of narcotics and other problems of concern to teenagers and other young people.

Following their tour, Presley privately advised that he has volunteered his services to the President in connection with the narcotics problem and that Mr. Nixon had responded by furnishing him an Agent's badge of the Bureau of Narcotics and Dangerous Drugs. Presley was carrying this badge in his pocket and displayed it.

Presley advised that he wished the Director to be aware that he, Presley, from time to time is approached by individuals and groups in and outside of the entertainment business whose motives and goals he is convinced are not in the best interests of this country and who seek to have him to lend his name to their questionable activities. In this regard, he volunteered to make such information available to the Bureau on a confidential basis whenever it came to his attention. He further indicated that he wanted the Director to know that should the Bureau ever have any need of his services in any way that he would be delighted to be of assistance.

Presley indicated that he is of the opinion that the Beatles laid the groundwork for many of the problems we are having with young people by their filthy unkempt appearances and suggestive music while entertaining in this country during the early and middle 1960's. He advised that the Smothers Brothers, Jane Fonda, and other persons in the entertainment industry of their ilk have a lot to answer for in the hereafter for the way they have poisoned young minds by disparaging the United States in their public statements and unsavory activities.

Presley advised that he resides at 3764 Highway 51, South, Memphis, Tennessee, but that he spends a substantial portion of his time in the Beverly Hills, California - Las Vegas, Nevada, areas fulfilling motion picture assignments and singing commitments.

He noted that he can be contacted anytime through his Memphis address and that because of problems he has had with people tampering with his mail, such correspondence should be addressed to him under the pseudonym Colonel Jon Burrows.

- 2 -

CONTINUED - OVER

145

M. A. Jones to Bishop Memo
RE: ELVIS PRESLEY

It should be here noted following their tour and prior to their departure from the building, Mr. Morris indicated that Presley had been recently selected by the Junior Chamber of Commerce as one of the "ten outstanding men" in the United States and that of these ten in a ceremony to be held in Memphis sometime in January, 1971, Presley would be named as the "most outstanding" of the ten. According to Morris, similar recognition was afforded President Nixon some 25 years ago and the late President Kennedy was also a recipient of this award.

Morris observed that he has known Presley for many years, that despite his manner of dress, he is a sober, clean minded young man who is good to his family and his friends and who is very well regarded by all, including the law enforcement community in the Memphis Tennessee, area where he was raised and still resides.

Presley, Morris, and their party expressed appreciation for the courtesies extended them.

OBSERVATION:

Presley did give the impression of being a sincere, young man who is conscious of the many problems confronting this country. In view of his unique position in the entertainment business, his favorable comments concerning the Director and the Bureau, and his offer to be of assistance as well as the fact that he has been recognized by the Junior Chamber of Commerce and the President, it is felt that a letter from the Director would be in order.

RECOMMENDATION:

That the attached letter to Presley be approved and sent.

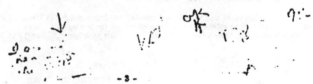

- 3 -

146

((Rev. 2-3-59)

UNITED STATES DEPARTMENT OF JUSTICE
FEDERAL BUREAU OF INVESTIGATION

1 - U. S. ATTORNEY, MEMPHIS
  (ATTENTION: AUSA GLEN GARLAND REID, JR.)
Copy to: 1 - U. S. ATTORNEY, SOUTHERN DISTRICT OF NEW YORK)
  (ATTENTION: AUSA JEFF LAUGENER)

Report of: SA [redacted] b7C   Office: MEMPHIS
Date: AUGUST 2, 1977

Field Office File #: 87-16994   Bureau File #: 87-143601

Title: FREDERICK N. P. PRO;
ELVIS A. PRESLEY - VICTIM

Character: INTERSTATE TRANSPORTATION OF STOLEN PROPERTY -
FRAUD BY WIRE

Synopsis:
the cardex system was never put in the Jetstar; [redacted] states b7D
           The only work done on PRESLEY's Jetstar was
minimal maintenance.   b3

claims only pre-flight examinations were performed on the
Jetstar plus some on the Airworthiness-Directive note.

[large redaction]   b7D

-P-

U.S. GPO:1975-0-579-041   73

NE 87-16994

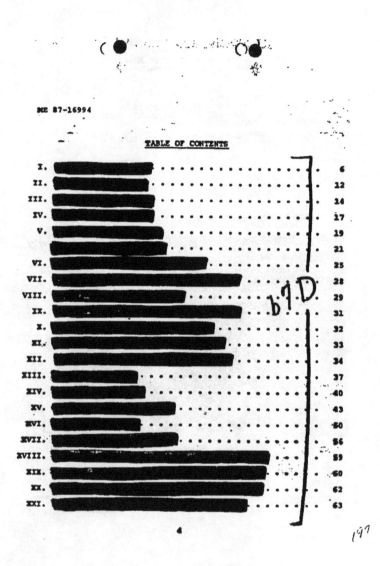

TABLE OF CONTENTS

b7D

4

197

ME 87-16994

(Table of Contents Continued)

5

FD-263 (Rev. 7-13-75)

FEDERAL BUREAU OF INVESTIGATION

REPORTING OFFICE	OFFICE OF ORIGIN	DATE	INVESTIGATIVE PERIOD
NEW YORK	MEMPHIS	NOV 3 1977	10/18-10/21/77

TITLE OF CASE	REPORT MADE BY	TYPED BY
CHANGED RAYMOND W. BAZNER - FUGITIVE; GABRIEL ROBERT CAGGIANO - FUGITIVE; PHILLIP KARL KITZER, Jr. - FUGITIVE; (TITLE CONT'D COVER PAGE B)	b7C	

CHARACTER OF CASE

ITSP - FBW - MF - CONSPIRACY

11-21-77

Title is changed to reflect the true name of subject as FREDERICK PETER PRO, aka (TN) Alfredo Proc. This subject was previously carried as FREDERICK N. P. PRO. Subject stated his birth certificate erroneously shows his name as ALFREDO PROC, but said his true name is FREDERICK PETER PRO.

REFERENCES

NYlet to Memphis, 10/11/77.
MEtel to the Bureau, 10/13/77.
NYtel to the Bureau, 10/18/77.-19
NYtel to the Bureau, 10/21/77.

—RUC—

ACCOMPLISHMENTS CLAIMED	☐ NONE				ACQUIT-TALS	CASE HAS BEEN:		
CONVIC.	AUTO.	FUG.	FINES	SAVINGS	RECOVERIES		PENDING OVER ONE YEAR ☐YES ☐NO	
		1					PENDING PROSECUTION OVER SIX MONTHS ☐YES ☐NO	

APPROVED	SPECIAL AGENT IN CHARGE	DO NOT WRITE IN SPACES BELOW

COPIES MADE:

1 - Bureau (87-143601)
1 - USA, SDNY (ATT: AUSA JACOB LAUFER)
1 - USA, Memphis
1 - Indianapolis (87-22720) (INFO)
1 - New York (196-66)
(COPIES CONT'D COVER PAGE B)

87-

REC-6
EX-10

4 NOV 7 1977

Dissemination Record of Attached Report		Notations
Agency		
Request Recd.		
Date Fwd.		
How Fwd.		
By		

DEC 1 1977

—A—
COVER PAGE

87-143601-23

150

750 (3-1-79)

FEDERAL BUREAU OF INVESTIGATION
FOIPA DELETED PAGE INFORMATION SHEET

_4_ Page(s) withheld entirely at this location in the file. One or more of the following statements, where indicated, explain this deletion.

☒ Deleted under exemption(s) _(b)(7)(D)_ with no segregable material available for release to you.

☐ Information pertained only to a third party with no reference to you or the subject of your request.

☐ Information pertained only to a third party. Your name is listed in the title only.

☐ Document(s) originating with the following government agency(ies) _____
_____ , was/were forwarded to them for direct response to you.

_____ Page(s) referred for consultation to the following government agency(ies); _____
_____ as the information originated with them. You will be advised of availability upon return of the material to the FBI.

_____ Page(s) withheld for the following reason(s):
_____
_____

☐ For your information: _____
_____

☒ The following number is to be used for reference regarding these pages:
_87-143601-2 p. 26-29_

```
XXXXXXXXXXXXXXXXXXXX
DELETED PAGE(S)
NO DUPLICATION FEE
FOR THIS PAGE
XXXXXXXXXXXXXXXXXXXX
```

XXXXXX
XXXXXX
XXXXXX

FBI/DOJ
37

151

FD-65 (Rev. 8-5-74)

UNITED STATES GOVERNMENT

Memorandum

TO : Director, FBI (87-143601)
     Att: Special Investigative Division

DATE: 2/13/78

FROM : SAC, MEMPHIS (P)

SUBJECT: FREDERICK N. P. PRO, aka -FUGITIVE;
         ET AL;
         ELVIS A. PRESLEY - VICTIM
         ITSP; FBW; MF; CONSPIRACY

☒ Initial Submission 86128
☐ Supplements FD-65 dated
☐ Photograph not needed

Indicate following:
☐ Extremist (Black)
☐ Extremist (White)
☐ Rev. Act.
☐ Other Security background
☐ None of these

8

Caution	MKE	Name				NAM	Sex	SEX	Race	RAC
☐		FREDERICK N. P. PRO					M		W	
Place of Birth				POB	Birth Date	DOB	Height	HGT	Weight	WGT
Pennsylvania					8/2/26		6'		181	
Eye Color	EYE	Hair Color	HAI	FBI No.		FBI	Skin Tone			SKN
BRN		GRAY/BRN			67C		OLIVE			
Scars, Marks, Tattoos, etc.										SMT
		FUGITIVE CARDS PREPARED								
NCIC Fingerprint Classification		Date		FPC Identifying Number		MNU	Social Security #			SOC
								67C		
Operator's License Number			OLN	Operator's License State		OLS	Year Expire		67C	OLY
							74			

Offense Charged OFF	ITSP; MAIL FRAUD; FRAUD BY WIRE; CONSPIRACY				
U. S. Code, Title and Section	Title 18, Sections 1341, 2, 2314, 1343, 371				
Warrant Issued By	USDJ HARRY WELLFORD	2/10/78	ROV	F.O. File #	OCA
				196-21	
Date PBV or Bond Default Case Referred to Office					
Miscellaneous Including Bond Recommended		MIS	Fingerprint Classification (Henry System)		
$50,000 secured over and above $75,000 posted					

LICENSE PLATE AND VEHICLE INFORMATION						
License Plate Number	LIC	State	LIS	Year Expires	LIY	License Plate Type	LIT
Vehicle Identification #	VIN	Year	VYR	Make VMA	Model VMO	Style VST	Color VCO
Aliases						
ALFREDO PROC, FRED PROC						
NCIC #		NIC				
W182605124			2 - Bureau / 1 - Memphis			

FUGITIVE INDEX
56 MAR 11 1978

87-143601-46

FBI/DOJ

152

IN THE UNITED STATES DISTRICT COURT
FOR THE WESTERN DISTRICT OF TENNESSEE
WESTERN DIVISION

UNITED STATES OF AMERICA

V.   CR-77-20281-01

FREDERICK P. PRO

ORDER DIRECTING ISSUANCE OF WARRANT OF ARREST
AND THE POSTING OF ADDITIONAL CASH BOND

On October 31, 1977, the defendant, Frederick P.
Pro, signed Bail Reform Act Form No. 2 in this District.
After a hearing concerning the bond in this matter, this
Court imposed several conditions of release, including
the execution of a bond in the amount of $75,000.00, cash
or surety bond. Further, this Court directed that the
defendant Pro was to report in person each Tuesday and
Friday by 12:00 noon to the Federal Pre-Trial Services
Agency, Southern District of New York, where he was to
sign the Agency's register.

On February 10, 1978, the United States orally
moved this Court to issue a warrant for the arrest of the
defendant Pro and to cancel his bond, in light of the fact
that the defendant Pro had not reported to the Federal
Pre-Trial Services Agency in New York as directed. In light
of all the facts and circumstances of this case and for
good cause shown, it is ORDERED that a warrant issue for
the arrest of the defendant, Frederick P. Pro. The Court
further finds that the bond heretofore posted by the
defendant Pro is now insufficient. Therefore, it is
ORDERED that the defendant Pro execute a further and
additional cash bond in the amount of $50,000.00.

ENTER: This 15th day of February, 1978.

_____
UNITED STATES DISTRICT JUDGE

APPROVED:

W. J. MICHAEL CODY
United States Attorney

W. Hickman Ewing, Jr.
Assistant United States Attorney

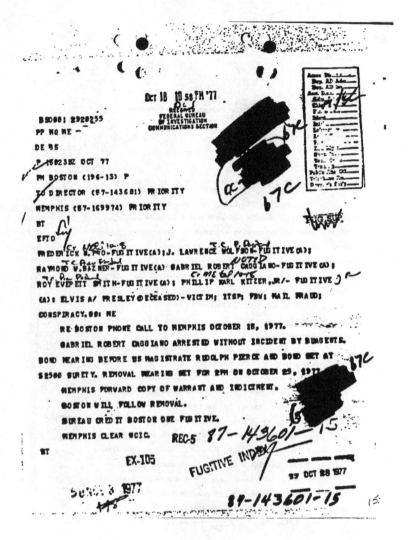

OCT 18 18 58 FM '77
RECEIVED
FEDERAL BUREAU
OF INVESTIGATION
COMMUNICATIONS SECTION

BS0001 2920255
PP HQ ME –
DE BS
P 150235Z OCT 77
FM BOSTON (196-13) P
TO DIRECTOR (87-143681) PRIORITY
MEMPHIS (87-169974) PRIORITY
BT
EFTO
FREDERICK W. PRO-FUGITIVE(A); J. LAWRENCE WOLFSON-FUGITIVE(A);
RAYMOND W. BAZNER-FUGITIVE(A); GABRIEL ROBERT CAGGIANO-FUGITIVE(A);
ROY EVERETT SMITH-FUGITIVE(A); PHILLIP KARL KITZER,JR/- FUGITIVE
(A); ELVIS A/ PRESLEY(DECEASED)-VICTIM; ITSP; FBW; MAIL FRAUD;
CONSPIRACY.00: ME

RE BOSTON PHONE CALL TO MEMPHIS OCTOBER 18, 1977.

GABRIEL ROBERT CAGGIANO ARRESTED WITHOUT INCIDENT BY SBAGENTS.
BOND HEARING BEFORE US MAGISTRATE RUDOLPH PIERCE AND BOND SET AT
$2500 SURETY. REMOVAL HEARING SET FOR 2PM ON OCTOBER 25, 1977.
MEMPHIS FORWARD COPY OF WARRANT AND INDICTMENT.

BOSTON WILL FOLLOW REMOVAL.

BUREAU CREDIT BOSTON ONE FUGITIVE.

MEMPHIS CLEAR NCIC.

BT

REC-5 87- 143601- 15

EX-105

FUGITIVE INDEX

37 OCT 28 1977

87-143601-15

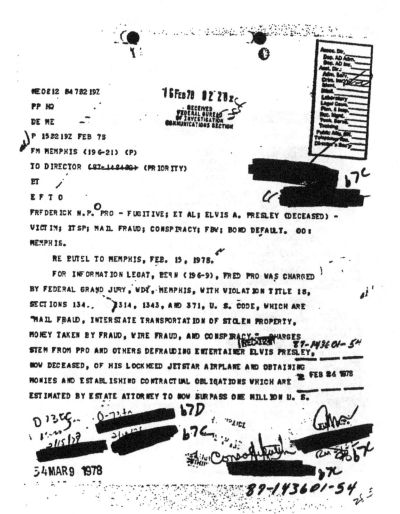

NE0212 84 782 19Z

PP HQ

DE ME

P 15 2219Z FEB 78

FM MEMPHIS (196-21) (P)

TO DIRECTOR (87-142400) (PRIORITY)

BT

E F T O

FREDERICK N.P. PRO - FUGITIVE; ET AL; ELVIS A. PRESLEY (DECEASED) - VICTIM; ITSP; MAIL FRAUD; CONSPIRACY; FBW; BOND DEFAULT. OO: MEMPHIS.

RE BUTEL TO MEMPHIS, FEB. 15, 1978.

FOR INFORMATION LEGAT, BERN (196-9), FRED PRO WAS CHARGED BY FEDERAL GRAND JURY, WDT, MEMPHIS, WITH VIOLATION TITLE 18, SECTIONS 134., 2314, 1343, AND 371, U. S. CODE, WHICH ARE MAIL FRAUD, INTERSTATE TRANSPORTATION OF STOLEN PROPERTY, MONEY TAKEN BY FRAUD, WIRE FRAUD, AND CONSPIRACY. CHARGES STEM FROM PRO AND OTHERS DEFRAUDING ENTERTAINER ELVIS PRESLEY, NOW DECEASED, OF HIS LOCKHEED JETSTAR AIRPLANE AND OBTAINING MONIES AND ESTABLISHING CONTRACTUAL OBLIGATIONS WHICH ARE ESTIMATED BY ESTATE ATTORNEY TO NOW SURPASS ONE MILLION U. S.

FD-302 (REV. 3-8-77)

FEDERAL BUREAU OF INVESTIGATION

1

Date of transcription   3/24/81

Oelwein, Iowa, telephone number ████████████ provided the
following information:

██████████ stated that in February of 1979, he traveled
to Atlantic City, New Jersey, to attend an antique car auction
sponsored by Kruse Auction Company. ████████ advised that he had
read about the auction during the first part of February, 1979,
in a newspaper entitled "Old Cars Weekly", which is published
in Iola, Wisconsin. ████████████ advised that the particular issue
of the newspaper that he read mentioned that the auction was
going to auction off a 1955 Chevrolet Corvette automobile, which
was owned by Elvis Presley.

██████████ advised that on February 17, 1979, he bid
$34,000 for this Chevrolet Corvette which supposedly belonged
to Elvis Presley, and his bid was accepted. ████████ stated
that the previous owner of the Corvette was ████████████████
who lived in West Chester, Pennsylvania. ████████ stated that
he did not meet ████████████ until after the sale of the
automobile.

██████████ advised that Kruse auctioneer definitely
purported the Chevrolet Corvette to be a car which was owned
by Elvis Presley. ████████ advised that the Corvette was
displayed in a roped-off area which had spotlights shining
on the car, and Elvis Presley's music was being played in the
background. ████████ advised that the auction was also selling
xeroxed copies of the bill of sale of the automobile, which
indicated that the Corvette was purchased from Don Allen Chevrolet
in New York City on January 18, 1955, by Elvis Presley. ████
advised the Vehicle Identification Number for the Corvette was
VE55S001102. ████████ stated that the odometer reading for the
automobile at the time he purchased the car was 45,731 miles.
████████ stated that the auctioneer, whose name he does not
recall, told him that the Corvette was restored by someone after

| Investigation on | 3/12/81 | at | Oelwein, Iowa | File # | Omaha 87B-18813-5 |

by   SA ████████████████████████

Date dictated   3/18/81

153

OM 87B-18813   2

Presley had owned it and during the restoration, a bill of
sale was discovered beneath the seat of the Corvette. This
bill of sale is the bill of sale that indicated Elvis
Presley had purchased the vehicle in New York City on
January 18, 1955.

           advised that he has the original invoice
for the car and also the original bill of sale, and both
of these documents indicate that the Corvette formerly
belonged to Elvis Presley.

           advised that he received the title to
the Corvette from _____ stated that
no one at the auction mentioned anything about the possibility
of the car not being Elvis Presley's car. _____ advised
he had the car transported to Oelwein, Iowa, where he has
it in storage at the present time. _____ has color
photographs of Elvis Presley's Corvette and other antique
cars which were at the February, 1979, Kruse Auction in
Atlantic City, New Jersey.

           advised that _____ told him
that he had owned the car himself for about one year and that
he had shown the automobile at various shows and shopping
centers, and he would receive money for these showings.
_____ stated that he heard from someone that
paid $24,000 for the Corvette when he bought it.
advised the Corvette has a three-speed manual transmission
and a Wonder Bar radio in it. _____ advised that in the
September 25, 1979, issue of Old Cars Weekly an article
appeared which questioned the authenticity of the Corvette
because of the fact that the Corvette had a three-speed
manual transmission and a Wonder Bar radio in it. _____
stated the article indicated that these options were not
available at the time Presley purchased the vehicle.
_____ stated he realizes these options could have been
added to the car after Presley owned it; and the car may
still, in fact, be one of Elvis Presley's automobiles.
advised that he has a good title for the automobile, but he
wants to know if he has been defrauded by someone in the
purchase of this car.

b7D

154

OM 87B-18813   3

████████ stated that he previously contacted the
Iowa Attorney General's Office in Des Moines, Iowa, to have
them check to see if the Presley Corvette is a fraud;
however, the Attorney General's Office was unable to
determine this fact. ████████ stated that he checked with
General Motors and they determined that the Vehicle
Identification Number for the Corvette was the same number
of a Corvette which was manufactured and shipped to
Don Allen Chevrolet for sale. General Motors, according
to ████████ was not able to determine if the car was, in
fact, sold to Presley.

████████ stated he does not know if the car is
a fraud, but he is restricted in selling the car if it is.
████████ stated the car would be worth approximately $24,000
if it is not Elvis Presley's Corvette; however, it would
be worth alot more than $34,000 if it was, in fact, one
of Presley's automobiles. ████████ stated he has had several
calls from persons throughout the United States wanting to
buy the Corvette prior to the article appearing in the Old
Cars Weekly newspaper in September of 1979.

b7D

7-1b

REPORT
of the

FBI
LABORATORY

FEDERAL BUREAU OF INVESTIGATION
WASHINGTON, D. C. 20535

To:
SAC, Omaha (87B-18813)   May 15, 1981

FBI FILE NO. 87-153820·

LAB. NO. 10410038 D UI

Re: 1955 CHEVROLET CORVETTE CONVERTIBLE,
VIN VE55S001102, FORMERLY OWNED BY
ELVIS PRESLEY, VALUED AT $34,000;
ITSP (B)

Specimens received April 9, 1981

Q1   Don Allen Chevrolet car invoice #15208, dated
            1/18/55, for a 1955 Chevrolet Corvette, VIN VE
            55S001102

Result of Examination:

The typewriting appearing on specimen Q1 corresponds
to a pica style of type available on IBM, SCM, and Remington
typewriters, having a horizontal spacing of ten characters
to the inch. This typewriter is equipped with typebars, as
apposed to a printwheel or a single element.

Without an authentic form similar to specimen Q1,
it cannot be determined whether Q1 is an authentic car
invoice. However, some printing characteristics were noted
which are associated with producing fraudulent documents by
the offset printing process.

Specimen Q1 contains no watermark.

Specimen Q1 is being returned herewith. Photographs
are retained.

142

CAR INVOICE
95-303

CHEVROLET

DON ALLEN CHEVROLET
1775 BROADWAY
NEW YORK 19, N. Y.

15208

SOLD TO: **ELVIS PRESLEY**

ADDRESS: **1034 AUDOBON DRIVE**
MEMPHIS, TENN.

DATE **JAN.18,1955**

SALESMAN

MAKE	YEAR	MODEL	BODY STYLE	COLOR	CYL or CLCS	KEY NO.	SERIAL NUMBER AND/OR ENGINE NO.
CHEV.	1955	CORV.	CONV.	RED	N	44A7	VE558001102

INSURANCE COVERAGE INCLUDES

☐ FIRE AND THEFT ☐ PUBLIC LIABILITY - AMT.
☐ COLLISION - AMT. DEDUCT. ☐ PROPERTY DAMAGE - AMT.

OPTIONAL EQUIPMENT AND ACCESSORIES

GROUP	DESCRIPTION	PRICE
	195 H.P. "Turbo Fire V8"	
	3 Speed Manual Transmission	
	Wonderbar Radio (Signal Seeking)	
	Trunk Mat	
	Floor Mats	

PRICE OF CAR
FREIGHT AND HANDLING
OPTIONAL EQUIP. & ACCESS.

SALES TAX
LICENSE AND TITLE
TOTAL CASH PRICE   **3864.00**

FINANCING
INSURANCE
TOTAL TIME PRICE

SETTLEMENT:
DEPOSIT
CASH ON DELIVERY
USED CAR:
YEAR   MAKE
MODEL   BODY
SER. NO.
MTR. NO.
PAYMENTS:
        AT $
        AT $

NAME OF FINANCE COMPANY:

TOTAL   **3864.00**

PRINTED IN U.S.A.

1/18/55 4/27/

Rec'd From=
67D Evansdale Iowa

UNITED STATES GOVERNMENT

memorandum

DATE: 6/15/81

REPLY TO
ATTN OF: SAC, OMAHA (87B-18813) (P)

SUBJECT: CHANGED I. O.

$87B-18813$ b7C

1955 CHEVROLET CORVETTE CONVERTIBLE,
VIN VE55S00102, FORMERLY OWNED BY
ELVIS PRESLEY, VALUED AT $34,000
ITSP (B)
OO: Omaha

TO: SAC, ST. LOUIS

       Title marked Changed I. O. to add the name   b7C
of subject███████████

       Enclosed for each receiving office is one copy
of an invoice Number 15208 from Don Allen Chevrolet, 1775
Broadway, New York 19, New York, dated 1/18/55, for a
1955 Chevrolet Corvette convertible, sold to Elvis Presley,
1034 Audobon Drive, Memphis, Tennessee, for a total cash
price of $3,864.

       For the information of receiving offices,████████
purchased a 1955 Chevrolet Corvette convertible,
red in color, VIN VE55S00102, at the Kruse Antique Car
Auction in Atlantic City, New Jersey, on 2/19/79, for
the purchase price of $34,000. This vehicle was purported
to be a vehicle previously purchased and owned by Elvis
Presley of 1034 Audobon Drive, Memphis, Tennessee. Mr.
Presley, according to the only supporting document available,
a bill of sale, Number 15208, purchased the vehicle on or
about 1/18/55, from Don Allen Chevrolet, 1775 Broadway,
New York City, New York. The Don Allen Chevrolet Company
of New York City has been out of business since 1966.

2-St. Louis (Enc. 1)
2-Memphis (Enc. 1)
2-Newark (Enc. 1)
(2)Omaha
(8)

$87B-18813-13$

Searched _____
Serialized _____
Indexed _____
Filed _____

b7C

OPTIONAL FORM NO. 10
(REV. 7-76)
GSA FPMR (41 CFR) 101-11.1
5010-112

166

ON 87B-18813

███████████ read an article in the 9/25/79 issue
of "Old Cars Weekly" that questioned the authenticity of the
1955 Corvette due to the fact that the automobile has a
three-speed manual transmission and also a WonderBar station-
seeking radio. According to several Corvette authorities,
these options were not available in January of 1955. There
is also a question as to whether or not the Turbo Fire V8
engine was available in January of 1955.

The State Attorney General's Office from Des Moines,
Iowa, conducted a preliminary investigation in this matter
for ███████████ however, they were unable to prove or
disprove the authenticity of the invoice in question.

On 11/10/79 a letter was sent to ███████████
███████ West Chester, Pennsylvania, who
had sold the vehicle to ███████ at the Kruse Auction.
███████ attorney, ███████ advised the Attorney
General's Office by letter that ███████ had purchased the
vehicle in Atlantic City, New Jersey, during February of 1978,
from a Mr. ███████ Neponsit,
New York 11694, for a purchase price of $17,500. According
to ███████ attorney, the vehicle had been represented by
███████ as formerly belonging to Elvis Presley; and ███████
had made available the invoice document in question.

On 10/11/79 contact was made with Attorney at Law
D. Beecher Smith, II, Suite 2000, Number One Commerce Square,
Memphis, Tennessee, telephone number (901) 525-1322, the
attorney handling the estate of Elvis Presley. Smith told
the Attorney General's Office from Des Moines, Iowa, that his
office would not be able to help in the investigation due to
the fact that most of the records per any business transactions
by Presley prior to 1973 were destroyed.

███████████ of Neponsit, New York, was interviewed
on 5/8/81, and he indicated that he was a collector of cars
and sold over 80 cars during the past 10 years through the
Kruse auctioneers. ███████ admitted buying captioned vehicle
for $4,000 from a New Jersey resident; and he, himself, spent
$10,000 in parts for the Corvette in order to refurbish it.
███████ advised he did not change the transmission of the
automobile, nor did he install a new radio in the car. ███████
was not able to provide the name of the individual who owned

b7C

b7D

2

167

CM 87B-18813

the car; however, he did indicate that he bought the car from
a man who lived in New Jersey. ▮▮▮▮ advised that the invoice,
or bill of sale that he received when he purchased the car
from the man in New Jersey, was sold to him with the car and
he laminated the invoice himself.

▮▮▮▮ stated that if he were able to positively prove
the car belonged to Elvis Presley, he would have been able to
sell it for $100,000; but, in fact, he sold the car to ▮▮▮
▮▮▮through the Kruse Auction for $17,500 and his profit
was less than $3,000 on the car.

To date, ▮▮▮▮▮▮▮ of West Chester,
Pennsylvania, has not been reached for interview by the FBI.

The Iowa Attorney General's Office at Des Moines,
Iowa, learned from the Department of Motor Vehicles for the
State of New Jersey that the captioned automobile was purchased by▮▮▮ on 2/16/78 from ▮▮▮▮
of▮▮▮▮▮ Basking Ridge, New Jersey, telephone
number▮▮

The original of the enclosed invoice was examined
by the Document Section of the FBI Laboratory and it was noted
that there were several corrections made on the document and
also it appeared as though there were areas in which the lines
and several letters had been retouched as is often the case
in the production of counterfeit documents. The typewriter
used to prepare the document and the Correcto-type tape used
to make typewriter corrections were both available commercially
in 1955. The FBI Laboratory would need an original Don Allen
Chevrolet car invoice to compare ▮▮▮▮invoice to in order
to specifically state whether or not the document was a fraud.

LEADS

    ST. LOUIS DIVISION

    AT ST. LOUIS, MISSOURI

        Will contact the Chevrolet Manufacturing Plant, Corvette
Division, and attempt to determine if captioned 1955 Chevrolet

OM 87B-18813

Corvette automobile with VIN VE55S00102 could have been manufactured with the following optional equipment and accessories:

      1) A 195 horsepower "Turbo Fire V8" engine.

      2) A three-speed manual transmission.

      3) A WonderBar signal-seeking radio.

MEMPHIS DIVISION

AT MEMPHIS, TENNESSEE

      Will contact D. Beecher Smith, II, Attorney at Law,
Suite 2000, Number One Commerce Square, Memphis, Tennessee,
telephone number (901) 525-1322, the attorney handling the
estate of Elvis Presley, and determine from Mr. Smith if it
would possible to identify the insurance company used by
Presley to insure his automobiles and other vehicles.

      If the insurance company is identified and if a
representative office of that company is located in Memphis,
Tennessee, will contact the office to determine if captioned
vehicle is listed among the vehicles insured by Presley.

NEWARK DIVISION

AT BASKING RIDGE, NEW JERSEY

      Will interview ▮▮▮▮▮▮▮▮▮▮▮▮▮▮▮▮▮▮▮▮▮▮
telephone number ▮▮▮▮▮▮▮▮ to determine the facts
surrounding his purchase and subsequent ownership of captioned
automobile.

      Will determine how ▮▮▮▮▮ came into possession of the
enclosed invoice which he provided to ▮▮▮▮▮▮▮ when he
sold the car to ▮▮▮▮

      Will determine from ▮▮▮▮▮ whom he purchased the
vehicle from and what he paid for the car when he bought it.

4

164

OM 87B-18813

   Will determine from ████████ if he altered or
renovated the automobile in any way while he owned it, and   b7C
will obtain copies of any documents ████████ might have
which would support a claim that the vehicle was formerly
owned by Elvis Presley.

5*

170

ABOUT THE EDITOR

Thomas Fensch is the author or editor of over 20 books of nonfiction published since 1970. His books include:

Steinbeck and Covici: The Story of a Friendship
Conversations With John Steinbeck
Conversations With James Thurber
Oskar Schindler and His List:
    The Man, the Book, the Film,
    The Holocaust and Its Survivors
    Associated Press Coverage of a
      Major Disaster:
    The Crash of Delta Flight 1141;
Of Sneetches and Whos and the Good Dr. Seuss:
    Essays on the Writings and Life of
Theodor Geisel

New Century Books by Thomas Fensch include:

The Man Who Was Dr. Seuss:
    The Life and Work of Theodor Geisel
The Man Who Was Walter Mitty:
    The Life and Work of James Thurber
U.S. Military Plans for the Invasion of Japan

Thomas Fensch holds a doctorate from Syracuse University and lives near Houston, Texas.

CPSIA information can be obtained
at www.ICGtesting.com
Printed in the USA
BVHW041353161222
654409BV00019B/44